the breakup monologues

the breakup monologues

The Unexpected Joy of Heartbreak

Rosie Wilby

GREEN TREE

LONDON • OXFORD • NEW YORK • NEW DELHI • SYDNEY

GREEN TREE
Bloomsbury Publishing Plc
50 Bedford Square, London, WC1B 3DP, UK
29 Earlsfort Terrace, Dublin 2, Ireland

BLOOMSBURY, GREEN TREE and the Green Tree logo are trademarks
of Bloomsbury Publishing Plc

First published in Great Britain 2021
Copyright © Rosie Wilby, 2021

Rosie Wilby has asserted her right under the Copyright, Designs and Patents Act,
1988, to be identified as Author of this work

A catalogue record for this book is available from the British Library

Library of Congress Cataloguing-in-Publication data has been applied for

ISBN: HB: 978-1-4729-8230-8; TPB: 978-1-4729-9234-5;
ePub: 978-1-4729-8231-5; ePDF: 978-1-4729-8232-2

2 4 6 8 10 9 7 5 3 1

Typeset in Minion by Deanta Global Publishing Services, Chennai, India
Printed and bound in Great Britain by CPI Group (UK) Ltd, Croydon CR0 4YY

To find out more about our authors and books visit www.bloomsbury.com
and sign up for our newsletters

To outsiders, eccentrics, mavericks and all those who have been 'dumped' in a broader sense.

Contents

Introduction

Heartbreak is universal. Whether you are male, female, trans, non-binary, gay, straight, bisexual, pansexual, polyamorous, monogamous, young, old or somewhere in between, we all seem to navigate a similarly emotionally perilous happy-sad terrain in the unfortunate (or as it turns out sometimes, fortunate)[1] event that we have been dumped.[2]

But if you *really* want to know about breakups…you should ask a lesbian.

Yes. That's right. A lesbian.

I don't mean you should just rock up to a lesbian bar and start quizzing the first comfortably-shoed woman you see about ghosting, conscious uncoupling, rebound flings, heartbreak, addiction, serial monogamy, loneliness, grief, attachment theory, anti-love drugs, rebirth, transformation, personal growth and all the other sorts of things you're going to be reading about in this book. For a start, you'll be hard pushed to find a lesbian bar. Most of them have closed down.[3]

---

1   Sarah Ferguson, Duchess of York, or 'Fergie' to Brits of a certain age, probably dodged a bullet when she and Prince Andrew divorced in 1996. Recently, his longstanding links with an alleged sex trafficker have been exposed.

2   My Facebook friend Helen tells me that the therapeutic term for 'dumped' is actually 'narcissist discard' and 'reflects the values of the dumper and not the worth of the dumpee'. She likens her escape from life with a narcissist to a briskly-curtailed holiday on 'one of those beaches in Indonesia covered in landfill. On one level the brochure tells you it's idyllic. So you ignore the toxic waste. Then suddenly you're sent home. You wake up on a British beach. It's a massive shock. It's crisper. But true. Fresh air, living fish, reality…and after a good walk you can treat yourself to chips.'

3   I call this 'the paradox of progress'. As we become more accepted into mainstream society, there may arguably be less of an urgent need for safe spaces where we can hold hands or have a little kiss without getting beaten up. But it does mean that there's no longer anywhere to actually go and meet other gays.

No. I mean that lesbians are the unofficial, unrecognised world champions of breakups. Statistically speaking, we go through more breakups in a lifetime than anyone else.[4] So we have figured out how to do it kindly(ish).[5] Time and time again, I hear stories, studies and polls that suggest that we stay super-close friends[6] with an ex more frequently than anyone else. After all, it's a small community…and sometimes there's nobody else to be friends with.

So trust me when I say I've got some relevant life experience and a useful perspective on this topic – useful for lots of people.

Straight women! I've got your back. I know how it feels to get dumped as a woman.

Straight men! I've got your back too. I know how it feels to get dumped *by* a woman.

And queer people. I've got your back too, because you're my family and I love you. Simple.

So who the hell is *this* lesbian telling you to read her book?

I'm a professional comedian, radio presenter and compulsive serial monogamist. In 2016, I started obsessively exploring breakups in my work. I was concerned that perhaps I had been wasting years and years of my life expending so much energy on relationships that did not endure. Surely *real* love was supposed to last? I was on a quest to figure out how to finally settle down and stay with my awesome new partner. Let's call her Girlfriend.

It may seem odd how much of this book about breakups I spend talking about a relationship I'm trying, fighting[7] even, to stay *in*. But to me, breaking up and staying together are simply two sides of the same coin. They are a flick of a switch apart, separated only by one fleeting moment of madness, or perhaps clarity. They are as intertwined as the

---

4   According to the Office of National Statistics, female couples account for around three-quarters of same-sex divorces in the UK. This pattern seems to hold around the world. One *Curve Magazine* article even suggests that, in Australia, lesbians are 250 per cent more likely to divorce than straight couples! I'll explore the reasons for this later.
5   I once suggested on BBC *Woman's Hour* that 'if older lesbians ruled the world, we would have global peace.' I got a few tweets about that one. I still stand by it.
6   American poet Andrea Gibson even purchased a home with her ex.
7   When I say I'm 'fighting' to stay in my relationship, I'm not fighting with Girlfriend so much as with myself. If you've been a bit hooked on the rollercoaster drama of breakups and serial monogamy, often mining those highs and lows for creative inspiration, then your new settled life is still informed by the thing you were addicted to, by the lack of it, by your abstinence from it. Like any drug.

wayward sun-browned stems of ivy that creep up from our neighbour's garden and are slowly but surely obscuring the view from our bedroom window. And sometimes we ourselves can become entangled with the strands of our relationships in unhealthy ways that obscure our view. Sometimes, like it or not, it is time for a spot of pruning.

After touring a solo show all about my own most painful separation, somewhat ironically titled *The Conscious Uncoupling*, I began speaking to other comedians, authors and academics about heartbreak. Initially this was a live chat show called *The Breakup Monologues*. I had no real plans for it. I would probably start writing and touring another solo show about something else entirely. I would resume grinding away on the comedy circuit. But the discussions were so interesting and fun that I thought I really had better start recording them for a podcast. A new journey began. I wanted to get to the 'who, what, when and how' of breakups...and, more pertinently, the 'why'? Why the hell do we do this to one another?

Grounds for Divorce

Under Turkish fifteenth-century law, a woman had the freedom to divorce her husband if he did not provide her with enough coffee.

In the twenty-first century, relationships are more likely to end due to one of the 'big seven reasons' identified by my friend, the author, nurse and counsellor Kathy Labriola:

- Sexual problems (including mismatched libidos and affairs)
- Incompatibility around money
- Domestic issues arising from living together
- Drug and alcohol addiction
- Untreated mental health conditions
- Abuse (physical, verbal or emotional)
- Conflicts over autonomy and intimacy

Here's a rundown of my most significant breakups in reverse chronological order and an attempt to categorise them according to Kathy's list.

Nice Ex-Girlfriend (2011–2016): Technically, I suppose you could call this a **'sexual problems'** breakup. I was on the rebound when we met, still bouncing around all over the place, looking for answers, drowning in existential angst. Real intimacy felt like a wobbly, tearful step too far. Yet we established a loving bond, one that it seemed nonsensical to discard. After moving in together, we operated like a domestic dream team easily slipping into egalitarian roles and routines around bins, cooking, shopping and cleaning. As the years wore on, however, I missed the heady sensation of actually being 'in love'. I wondered if she did too. We talked, largely hypothetically, about non-monogamy. If your relationship is great in every way except sex, then can't you just 'outsource' that bit? The answer, for us, was ultimately 'no'. But we remain friends.

Some people would describe my time with Nice Ex-Girlfriend as a 'sorbet' relationship, a palate cleanser in between more sexually intense and emotionally precarious partnerships full of flavour and danger. But that seems too dismissive of a five-year connection, during which I started to learn about companionship, respect and mutual support, about better articulating one's needs to a partner…and occasionally even listening to theirs.

Secretive Ex-Girlfriend (2006–2011): So…*this* is the one I wrote a show about. In the unfurling moments of 2011, just as the vapour trails of the New Year's fireworks faded, I was dumped by email. I regularly joke onstage that I felt much better once I had corrected her spelling and punctuation…and changed the font. 'Breakup' in Wingdings is far more palatable.

But, in reality, I spent the entirety of my subsequent relationship trying to solve the mystery of what had happened. It took several years for Facebook, an unexpected truth-teller, to reveal that there had been an undeclared overlap between me and a new partner. For all her denials, my paranoia over the sad, icy Christmas holidays had been well-founded after all.

So that makes this another **'sexual problems'** breakup, right?

But the truth is not quite so simple. The internalised homophobia and shame linked to both of our mutually exacerbated **'untreated mental health conditions'** also played their part in dismantling what could have been a sweet, euphoric fling. I mistook passionate attraction for potential long-term commitment. I thought we were having such a lovely time that we had to stay together, compatible or not. I fought for it at all costs. And what costs they were.

She was not out to her parents. I struggled with the invisibility that entailed. Although she did once try to reassure me by saying that her parents had enjoyed the film *Brokeback Mountain*, I wasn't sure this gave the best sense of how well gay relationships can turn out. The years drifted by with no sign of progress, no recognition, no acceptance. I was frozen in time, a dirty secret. I couldn't move forward with my own life. We couldn't live together or have a child or a dog or do any of the things that 'normal' couples did.

I should have been relieved to receive the email and be put out of my misery. I wasn't. Our old favourite Lucinda Williams and Richard Hawley songs rang in my ears for months in a distorted, howling remix.

Looking back, I feel more empathy for her predicament. She mistreated me. However, she, in turn, was mistreated by a silly, prejudiced world that stood in the way of her authenticity.

She is the only ex who has ever enforced a 'no contact' rule. There was just too much pain on both sides.

Agoraphobic Ex-Girlfriend (2001–2003): This volatile breakup story slaloms between a whole number of reasons, from '**untreated mental health conditions**' to '**incompatibility around money**' to even more '**sexual problems**'. We met on London's acoustic music scene in the noughties when I was working as a singer songwriter. We bonded at a basement venue called The Kashmir Klub over the fact that our guitars were the same colour and began touring together…and fucking.

Her illness manifested in a strange way. She often made it to gigs. But only if she could park her car as close to the venue exit as possible, so that it almost became a temporary back porch, her escape vehicle ready and waiting for the moment we finished performing. Fortunately her skills in parking-fine avoidance were almost on a par with her enviable musical ability.

Yet when I wanted to see her to just hang out together and do girlfriend-y things, her undiagnosed anxieties seemed to kick in. She was 'ill' and couldn't make it. I was forever being stood up, waiting and waiting. 'How can you "go out" with someone who doesn't go out?' I moaned to any friends who would listen.

One night we bravely attempted to stay overnight at a festival. Once we got into our tent, it turned out that she was also claustrophobic. We were awake for hours alternating between zipping and unzipping the tent flap to combat each of the anxieties in turn, before driving back to London in the early hours.

When I became bored of waiting around for her and frustrated with eking out a living from sporadic gigs and fluctuating quarterly royalty payments, I got a job in music PR. It was just a temporary maternity-cover position. It was not a big deal. But she seemed to feel betrayed and retaliated by busying herself with a secret online flirtation with an old flame rekindled via the website Friends Reunited.[8]

'We met up and kissed. I'm sorry, I don't want to see her again. Don't break up with me,' she pleaded over the phone as I curled up in bed feeling like I'd been punched in the guts.

One morning at her place, while she was still in bed, a mobile phone beeped. It wasn't mine or hers. I whirled around to spot an offending bulge in the pocket of her denim jacket, hanging on the door…the spare phone, the common philanderer's trick. I removed it, glancing momentarily at the lusty text displayed on the screen, and threw it down sanctimoniously onto the pillow next to her. Or at least I tried to. Instead, the phone settled on a more aggressive flight path and clocked her right on the eyebrow.

'Ow!…What the…?…Oh…Oh shit…'

Although the romantic relationship was irreparably damaged, she was, unlike Secretive Ex-Girlfriend, demonstrably sorry for the hurt she caused. We have stayed in contact ever since…or at least as much as the agoraphobia allows.

Boozy Ex-Girlfriend (1996–2000): It was the nineties. We were in our twenties, starting out on our professional lives in London. Everyone went to work drunk…didn't they?

This breakup immediately sounds like it should come under '**drug and alcohol addiction**', a problem that I had barely recognised as such. I happily joined in with the partying. She was such a fun, affectionate

---

8   Online flirting, unless on a designated dating site, was quite unusual in 2002. Or so I thought.

drunk. I suppose it was just the times she poured herself a large tumbler of whisky at breakfast that I wondered if everything was alright.

But that's not really the whole story. A candle left burning on a flammable wicker bookcase one hungover morning acted as the catalyst that prematurely pushed us apart. We still loved each other, but perhaps not enough to recover together from the loss of our first adult home and all of our belongings. Fire is cruel and indiscriminate – my guitars melted and mangled into completely new shapes, our clothes disintegrated under a grimy layer of soot.

Our obliging friends all scrabbled around the backs of their wardrobes for old T-shirts, skirts and trousers that we could wear during the long weeks before we got an insurance payout and could start replacing things. However, some saw this as a good way to clear out all their old tat. One even gave me her Brownie uniform.

After a nomadic summer of sleeping on friends' floors and sporting horrific outfits, we went our separate ways. But we remained close and often commemorated 'fire day' by sending one another ironic gifts…of candles.

To file 'she got pissed and inadvertently burned our house down' under **'domestic issues arising from living together'** would feel like I'd be downplaying it a bit. It's hardly the equivalent of a spat about hoovering. So perhaps let's blame the booze after all.

Those are my 'big four' breakups. Before that, distance was often a factor as I moved around from my old hometown of Ormskirk[9] to University in York, then back again for the holidays and eventually to London for a film production trainee scheme. It was convenient to have this superficial reason to blame these early breakups on. In fact, other incompatibilities were at play.

Older Ex-Girlfriend (March 1993–June 1993): I couldn't possibly imagine anyone being as old[10] as twenty-six. It seemed so alluring, sophisticated and magical. She had a proper job up North as a teacher and knew how to cook meals that were not peanut butter toast.

---

9   Nondescript Lancashire market town. I always tell people it's a bit near Liverpool and a bit like Liverpool…if you take away *everything*.

10 Now I'm four years older than Girlfriend and it seems like no gap at all. It's all relative. We are ancient. I assumed I'd be dead by now. If I'd lived centuries ago, I would've been dead by this ripe old age. No wonder I've had so many breakups!

I would happily sit around, dreamily watching her do grownup things like chopping a courgette or wiping down a surface. When I had to leave for London, I spent my first few months living out the romantic idea of being heartbroken, writing love letters and listening to a lot of Kate Bush. I suppose you could put this down as a **'conflicts over autonomy and intimacy'** breakup. Because I had no idea yet what autonomy meant, I was actively looking for someone to be enthralled by. I was an idiot with no sense of self yet at all.

First-Ever Ex-Girlfriend (1990–1992): This entrepreneurial Scouser ditched her boring boyfriend and quit her boring job in a bank to become a DJ at Liverpool's leading lesbian club. She wore a leather jacket, had a mullet and was widely adored on the North-West scene. Yet whenever she visited me at uni, she felt insecure as she wasn't all 'academic' like my new friends. So I suppose this was a breakup around **'incompatibility around money'**, class and a sense of aspiration. However, ultimately, I was more inspired by her anarchic grab for freedom than she knew. Fuck respectable, sensible career plans. Express yourself and be authentic.

Ex-Boyfriend (1986–1987, 1988–1989): Of all the boys who drifted around me in my teens, there was one who kept popping up again. He was two years older and felt like one of my first proper friends. I initially stole him from one of my best mates, which cast me as something of a scarlet woman at school and was the beginning of all my troubles there. We nearly had sex on New Year's Eve. But Mum came to pick me up after the midnight service in Ormskirk and I left him with half a bottle of wine and a hard on. The precise reason for this breakup isn't on Kathy's list. I was gay! I don't feel completely comfortable in putting that down as another **'sexual problems'** split, even though technically that's the category it might come under.

The Importance of Stories

So far we've heard my stories. More recently, I have listened to a multitude of other people's funny, poignant, incredibly human tales of romantic woe. Although they may well fit into Kathy's categories, I have come to view every breakup as unique and as strangely beautiful as a snowflake. In 1969, the Swiss-American psychiatrist Elisabeth Kübler-Ross became famous for her theory of the five stages of grief – denial, anger, bargaining, depression and acceptance. Although she was writing about the emotions experienced by terminally ill patients, the model became widely viewed as a template for all forms of personal loss. Yet later in her life, Kübler-Ross expressed regret at documenting the stages in what was interpreted to be a linear and predictable pattern. Heartbreak is a peculiar chaos, one that we often feel guilt about wallowing in. It's not like the person has *actually* died.[11] And nor have we. But something precious has.

Largely speaking, I'm a believer in the old adage that 'tragedy plus time equals comedy' and that sharing these war stories is psychologically healthy. Amidst all the breakup bootcamps, motivational anti-heartbreak apps and divorce concierge services[12] that have sprung up in recent years, I still think that telling our story to other humans may be the best form of recovery. A study published in 2015 in the *Journal of Social and Personal Relationships* investigated the variation in how mental health is impacted after a breakup. One hundred and forty-six newly single men and women were asked to write narratives of significant events in their prior relationships. How people made meaning of these events through narrative seemed to influence their mental health afterwards. Not surprisingly, a more positive narrative ending corresponded with an 'adaptive resolution'. In other words, their trauma had been reduced.

But then a lecture by philosopher Lucy O'Brien, at a comedy conference I was also speaking at, made me start to question what I'm trying to achieve by sharing these stories onstage, so publicly. She wonders whether the comedian's invitation to others to laugh at them is a strange act of self-harm. Being laughed at is often hurtful. Is the invitation to laugh at one's past failings a way of gaining social credit in the present, a way to recoup some success? 'Look at how amazing I am *now* compared to that schmuck who got dumped'. Even so…isn't the result a zero-sum game if the teller of the joke is also the butt of it? She may have a point. In Hannah Gadsby's award-winning show *Nanette*,

---

11 Although it felt a bit like it when I was putting 'from and until' dates next to each girlfriend's nickname.

12 To help with all the breakup admin…like finding somewhere new to live.

she proposes that she will give up the career that she has built out of self-deprecating humour. She asks what self-deprecation means when it comes from somebody who already exists in the margins, and concludes that it is not humility but humiliation.

I can't imagine a life without comedy. It has become so woven into the fabric of my life and identity. So where has this obsession with using my comedy to explore heartbreak come from? BBC Radio 4 recently described me as the 'queen of breakups'. It's an odd accolade. Surely becoming super-skilled and experienced at breakups indicates a propensity to make bad romantic choices in the first place? Isn't love something that we should strive to do so well, so consciously and respectfully, that we subdue the more dramatic undulations of our own personal rollercoaster? I rather like this faux royal tag but it makes me wonder…what exactly am I trying to rule and conquer?

Prologue: The Butterfly Painting

'You look beautiful today.'

'Thanks, baby. You're a bit *into* me today, aren't you?'

'I'm always into you.'

'No you're not.'

'True.'

We are driving to a festival in Girlfriend's 'mid-life crisis' car, an electric-blue BMW convertible. Although the way she drives makes me wonder if you can still describe it as a 'mid-life' crisis if it ends up killing us. That would be an 'end-of-life' crisis...and quite a crisis at that. Never mind. The sun is shining. Our life is good. We have a fancy loft conversion. We go on ski holidays. We google things like, 'Can dogs eat mange tout?'[1] After two decades of scratching out a creative existence from gig to gig, first as a wistful indie songwriter and then as a wilfully grassrootsy comedian, I now get to live like a wanker because my libido went all aspirational on me and drew me to a partner with an actual job. However...

Three months shy of our three-year anniversary, shit has got real. Girlfriend and I have reached a refreshing level of frankness about the

---

1   Yes they can! Although apparently only in 'small amounts'. Anyway, our daft hound has no class. She prefers frozen peas.

fact that our mutual desire has waned. We have teetered and toppled over the parapet of honeymoon bliss and fallen to the ground below, stirred from the anaesthetising effects of the sexy brain chemicals that have propelled us along thus far with relative ease. Suddenly, we are acutely aware of the careers and friends that we have neglected during the happy haze. We have reached the stage where being in a relationship with a fellow human has become a massive pain in the arse…even though it is a largely excellent relationship that neither of us intends to leave.

Repeat. We are not going to break up. Not for the foreseeable. Not us.

In fact it is the first time I've reached this point and *not* been planning a daring, dramatic escape. Counting up the significant partners whom I probably would have married if it had been legally available to me all along, I am now on to my fifth 'wife'. That puts me on a multi-marriage par with Joan Collins. Already. At the age of forty-eight. She was sixty-eight when she married her final husband. If I *was* going to continue to be a slave to serial monogamy (and if you're reading this, darling Girlfriend, of course I'm not), I would have ample time to overtake her and catch up with Liz Taylor and her seven husbands (one of whom she married twice) or even Zsa Zsa Gabor and her tally of nine.

But I'm done with twisting. I think I'd like to stick. I've found a funny, sexy, generous[2] partner…even if she does have a ridiculous, knobby car. Surely if I left this one, I'd be breaking up with love altogether. It would be my endgame. And it is from this position of at least *wanting* to stay, of accepting the maddening claustrophobia of companionship, that I want to investigate why breakups continue to compel me so much.

Perhaps it is because breakups facilitate, and maybe even necessitate, transformation. In the wake of a separation, our peers allow us to reinvent ourselves. The rest of the time, they like us to stay fixed so that they can move around, and ahead of, us. But heartbreak is the golden ticket that circumvents this bullshit. Renewed and reborn, standing at

---

2   A 2010 study published in the *Journal of Psychological Science* asked 222 volunteers, all in relationships, to say their partners' names and then give words related to them. Not surprisingly, those who were fastest to link their partner-related vocabulary to negative words turned out to be more likely to have broken up when the researchers checked back in with them at a later date. I typically think of positive words to describe Girlfriend, unless we have just had a row. However, one of our friends recently joked that her girlfriend was her 'nemesis'. They separated a few weeks later.

the edge of the echoing canyon of our former frustrations, we shout, 'This is who I *am* now!' And we run and skip away from the parched carcasses of the old selves we have grown to hate.

For me, it has been during these fleeting, liberating gaps of singledom that I have really got shit done. I recorded and released an album. I launched a boutique music PR company. I started comedy. I wrote a book. Each time, I harnessed any lingering feelings of anger, sadness and confusion, and used them as energising forces for creativity, for moving forwards with new insights into my own shortcomings and foibles. I wonder if it is possible to do that much learning and actively *stay* in a relationship. I hope so. It must be, right? Or else all long-term couples would be codependent, emotionally stunted weirdos. Oh, hang on...

Don't get me wrong. My breakups have been hell. In the messy emotional aftermath of Secretive Ex-Girlfriend's clinical email, I felt trapped in the illusory impossibility of an endless staircase like the famous Penrose stairs published in the *British Journal of Psychology* in 1958, which in turn inspired Dutch artist Escher's mind-wrangling painting *Ascending and Descending*. I was trudging up and up and up, trying to get on with life, only to keep ending up back where I started, in tears and in pain. I was lost.

When I was a child, Dad guided me through the maze at the Tudor estate, Tatton Park. He told me that if I kept my right hand touching the hedge at all times, I would eventually navigate to the centre and out again. I was searching for some kind of logical, rational strategy like this to navigate out of heartbreak. I needed answers. Had she met someone else? How long had it been going on? And most important of all...

Why had I stayed for so long and passively waited for it to happen? Why didn't I *do* something?

And yet here I am in the passenger seat once again, both figuratively and literally. I glance over at Girlfriend, one hand nonchalantly caressing the steering wheel as she lifts a muscular arm to flick her red curls out of her eyes as they bounce around in the breeze, and think, 'I don't want to lose her, but, shit, I don't want to lose myself either.' Much as I might want to conform to the societal ideals of bourgeois, suburban coupledom, there's a wilder part of me that misses the old freedoms of being skint, dodging train fares and crafting homemade cards and gifts for transient lovers. A carefully curated CD-R wrapped in kitchen foil just wouldn't cut it now.[3] I sink down in my seat, eyeing the door. In my head, my comedy persona, the one I invented years ago that I thought was a bit of a dick until I realised it *was* actually me, thinks, 'I wonder if I'll die if I throw myself out at twenty-six miles per hour.'

* * *

Scratch scratch scratch.

It is 4 a.m. Girlfriend sighs.

Scratch scratch scratch.

'*Your* cat is being noisy.'

'Yes, I can hear that. I was awake anyway because *your* dog is taking up all of the bed.'

Cat is restless. An attention-seeking little minx, she revels in diverting me from spooning Girlfriend and Dog. She can sense that my love for her is less conditional than my affection for Dog. Our history dates back further, pre-Girlfriend. When Dog chews expensive sunglasses and underwear, I temporarily consider how I could conveniently lose her in the woods. Whereas Cat can scratch the furniture all she likes without denting my adoration…especially as the furniture mostly belongs to Girlfriend.

Cat frequently exploits this partiality. It has become habitual for me to tiptoe downstairs to the spare room in the early hours, with her tucked under my arm. Once she has me all to herself, she contentedly coils around the edge of my pillow and settles until breakfast time.

'Shhhh!'

This daft command, directed half-heartedly at Cat, is a waste of time. But I feel like it at least demonstrates some desire to stay in bed with Girlfriend.

Scratch scratch scratch.

I get up and slink towards the door.

'Oh…are you going?' murmurs Girlfriend.

I step back towards her and lean in, kiss her on the head and gently tap her three times on the shoulder. Tap tap tap. Our code for 'I love you.' She places her hand on mine for our stock reply. Tap tap-tap tap. 'So fucking much.'

---

3   Maybe this is why some of those transient lovers didn't last long. They were thinking, 'This cheap fucker didn't even buy me a birthday present.'

Cat has already racehorse-sprinted to the other room, the one occupied by my old bed. As her breathing slows and she instantly falls asleep, I whisper into her fur, 'You need to be nicer to your other mum. If you and I were living on our own together, we wouldn't be able to afford a house like this. You might not even have a garden or an outside space.' I wonder if really I am saying this as a reminder to myself.

I love Girlfriend. I really do. But I crave an uninterrupted night, one where we sleep separately...for the whole night. I am certain that she does too. Although it seems convenient to blame the pets, we just need that bit of distance from one another's snoring and fidgeting. Yet neither dare say it, for fear of casting some kind of sexless spell on the relationship.

But why on earth is segregated slumber such a taboo? Why is it presupposed to be a harbinger of doomed love? When Girlfriend and I first met, it was a delicious novelty to spend the night at her place, in her bed. Then go home for a proper comatose rest the following night. When there is less opportunity for sex, any brief window seems tantalising and irresistible, the thrill of a domestic deadline ramping things up even more.

'I've got a doctor's appointment in thirty minutes...time for a quickie?'

Living together, and being endlessly available to one another, changes all that. So why not shake things up with a 'sleep divorce'? Despite that unfortunate moniker, it works wonders for so many of my friends.[4]

In a slew of recent interviews to promote her podcast *Where Should We Begin*, renowned relationship therapist and author of *Mating in Captivity* Esther Perel encouraged the development of 'a personal intimacy with oneself as a counterbalance to the couple'. Where better to 'cultivate a secret garden' than in the giddiness of dreams? Meanwhile, a 2018 American study found that 62 per cent of couples would rather sleep alone. And among those who frequently did sleep alone, 78 per cent reported being completely happy with their partner. Mind you, this survey was conducted by a bed company who will, no doubt, be keen to sell twice as many beds.

Clang. Clang. Clang. Clang. Clang.

---

4   Forty-something women want some privacy for their perimenopausal night sweats.

The hourly nearby church bell alerts me to the fact that I've been awake, nonsense junk drifting through my head, for an hour. But it is sometimes these 5 a.m. thoughts that are the transformative ones. Among the 'brilliant new comedy routine' ideas that turn out to be gibberish in the cold glare of stage lights, sometimes there's a glimpse of something meaningful and a feeling of a burden being lifted.

And I whisper out into the darkness, 'What if we could view our relationships a bit like palindromes? What if at any point you could just fold the page over like one of those butterfly paintings you make as a child? Would that be a way of simultaneously looking back and forwards, of both learning from the past and striding decisively towards a new destination?'

I can picture it so clearly. The two halves of the butterfly are always the same but ever so slightly different once you smoosh them together, depending on the distribution of the paint. And how we view those two halves might alter depending on which parts of the pattern we decide to look at.

If I imagine a painting of my relationship with Girlfriend thus far, I am currently perched at the outer edge of the left wing. If I fold the page in on itself to imprint a sketch of the vibrancy and colour of the last three years onto the blank right-hand half of the paper, I'll be travelling in towards the butterfly body, towards our first dates and wildest sex. I'll be travelling backwards. Then I will pivot at the centre as the butterfly flaps its wings open. I'll be travelling forwards again. (Don't panic. I'll denote the timeline with 'B.G.' and 'A.G.' for 'Before Girlfriend' and 'After Girlfriend'. By 'After Girlfriend', I mean after we first met. I am hoping there is no actual life after Girlfriend. I'm four years older, less physically fit and way more sickly. I'm bound to die first. Hooray.)

I have long been a fan of mental time travel, having played three Dickensian ghosts of my romantic past, present and future in one of my solo shows. Perhaps I need these insightful apparitions to visit me again. Comedians are rubbish at living in the moment. It is part of the job to remove oneself, then clinically observe and deconstruct our lives from the sidelines. But maybe by viewing how the present is influenced by the past and simultaneously holds the key to the future, I can finally be present in it.

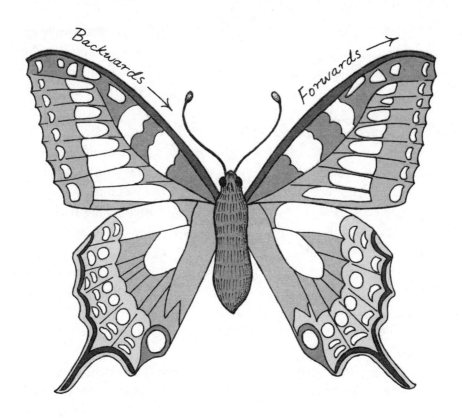

Hours later, Girlfriend pokes her head around the door to say that she's off to work.

'How did you sleep?'

Although her smile acknowledges the 4 a.m. interruption, I can tell that she wants me to play another of our little games. Recalling a favourite, seemingly nonsensical, expression of Girlfriend's mum Glenda, I do my best Welsh accent.

'Like a bomb.'

'Me too...Eventually! So...separate beds tonight?'

'Yes. I think so.'

Thank fuck for that.

Part One
Backwards

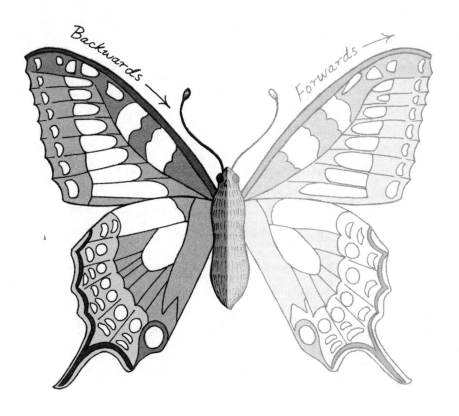

1

Wired for Love

2 years 9 months 3 weeks A.G. (After Girlfriend)

'Your PMT wasn't a problem for us in the early days.'

'That's because I was getting regular sex and I didn't get a chance to remember to be grumpy.'

'Maybe that's the answer!'

'Yes please.'

'Great. Who shall we get to fuck you?'

Sex is complicated. This is unfortunate…because sex seems intrinsic to the success and stability of a romantic relationship.

Pretty much every friend I have known endure a breakup has split because of sex. One or both people have sex with someone else. One or both people want to have sex with someone else. Or they simply no longer want to have sex with each other.[1]

What's even more alarming for a big old gay like me is that, according to surveys,[2] women are roughly twice as likely as men to become bored of a partner. So surely a *lesbian* partnership is a festering Petri dish of potential ennui, a ticking time bomb of indifference, a predictable portal to a pathological pattern of serial monogamy? No wonder lesbian divorces happen at several times the rate of gay male dissolutions.

Certainly, my life with Girlfriend has moved rapidly from marathon erotic workouts to herbal tea and home improvement.[3] 'Now *that's*

---

1   No wonder 'sexual problems' comes top of Kathy's list.
2   Good in Bed survey of 1418 men and 1923 women conducted by American sex researcher Kirsten Mark.
3   Whereas my gay male friends tell me that frequency of sex doesn't change much as you get older but the angles do.

sexy,' she giggles, as I bring the laundry basket downstairs to put on a wash. For once, though, I want to be a little bit *less* lesbian. I don't want to add Girlfriend to an expanding gaggle of (mostly) amicable former flings that I loved deeply but mysteriously fell out of lust with. At some social gatherings, it's easier to count who I *haven't* slept with. And that's not a good thing. I never set out to be some kind of ADHD sapphic Casanova.

But to really make my peace with long-term monogamous commitment and avoid yet another breakup, I need to understand my sexuality better. Once I can articulate my secret desires to myself, I can share them with Girlfriend. I really fancy her and still want to have sex with her. I'm just not sure I've ever quite worked out exactly what gets me going.

No surprise, then, that a recent tweet on *Diva* magazine's timeline caught my eye.

'What turns you on? Lesbians wanted for research into sexual arousal'.

Beneath this stirring header was a link to a brief application form to participate in a 'Sex Lab' at the University of Essex.

An accompanying article stated:

'Heterosexual and bisexual women display a curious pattern of sexual arousal: When shown explicit videos, they will display equal sexual arousal to videos featuring sexy men or sexy women.'

I have read about these experiments before. This was my chance to get involved. 'At the very least, I should get paid for an afternoon of watching porn. Hey ho, it's a hard life! I'm in,' I thought.

The article continued:

'Lesbians, however, show a marked preference for women in their sexual responses. This pattern has been found in a wide range of studies involving genital arousal, pupil dilation, viewing time and even brain activation patterns.'

These days, I would be chuffed to muster up any sexual response to anything at all.

I scrolled down to see a photo of a sort of techno-tampon, the 'sterilised vaginal probe' that I will have to insert once I have entered the privacy of the 'sealed booth'. In order to reassure potential participants of its unassuming size, the device was placed next to a plastic ruler. 'Awww,' I thought, observing that the sad little phallus barely reached the four-centimetre mark. I wondered if a more ample attachment might attract greater numbers of willing women.

An email from the sex lab pinged into my inbox a matter of minutes after I had submitted my application.

'When can you come in?'

They seemed a little desperate.

* * *

So here I am at the campus periphery being greeted by PhD student Luke. Shuffling towards me in a grey hoodie and jeans, he seems the kind of mild-mannered chap I can entrust with the task of measuring whether or not my vagina still has a pulse.

'Thanks for coming Rosie. How was your journey?'

'Fine, thanks.'

I wonder what kind of small talk one should engage in ahead of a sexy science experiment.

'Have you had many people in to participate?'

'Not so many today. It was manic yesterday though.'

At the end of a nondescript blue-hued corridor, we enter a room partitioned by some makeshift hardboard panelling. He leads me behind the panelling into a cramped cubicle containing a slightly reclining chair and a large television screen.

'So this is the probe,' he says, indicating a transparent sealed package containing the techno-tampon, wires protruding from it and leading under the partition to the computers on the other side.

'How does it work?'

Luke beams. I can tell that nobody else has asked this.

'Well…it bounces light against the vaginal walls and reads the illumination that bounces back. So it measures blood flow to the vagina.'

'Wow, fascinating.'

'We'll get you into position and once I've gone back out and you're ready, you can insert the probe. There's some lube over there on the shelf if you need it.'

I look over at the sachets and say, 'When in Rome!'

I immediately regret this little joke.

'Right…erm…I'll be talking to you on an intercom which is also just over there. Just press the button if you need to ask me anything.

Normally when I'm using the equipment, I just loosen my trousers and pull them slightly down. You don't need to completely undress.'

'Hahaha.'

I laugh awkwardly, while pondering where exactly he is inserting the techno-tampon and then realise that there must be an equivalent device for measuring penile arousal.[4]

On the chair, there's a bulge under some paper towels. I peek under the kitchen roll to see a pale blue horseshoe-shaped travel pillow.

'That's the best type of cushion for taking pressure off the probe. If you could sit on it in the chair, we need to position you so that your eyes are lined up with the camera so that we can measure your pupil dilation…So if you could move slightly to your right…and lift your head a little…yep, I think that's it.'

'So I need to keep my head in this position,' I say, sitting rigidly as if I'm in the midst of a stomach crunch.

'Yes. If possible.'

'I shouldn't wear my glasses then?'

'No. Not while you're watching the images. But you could pop them on the shelf over there so they're handy if you need them for reading the prompts in between.'

'And then put my head back in exactly the same position?'

'Yes.'

Good grief. This is getting complicated.

'Right OK. If you're happy, I'll leave you in here and go around to talk to you on the intercom.'

I loosen my jeans and tear open a sachet of lube.

It squirts all over my hand and I have way too much to slather all over the teeny-tiny techno tampon. Standing awkwardly with my trousers around my hips, I slide it in. It immediately slides right out and lands in the gusset of my pants.

Oh crap.

The intercom crackles into life.

'How's it going in there?'

I slide the techno tampon back in and immediately throw myself back down into position on the chair in order to keep hold of it this time.

---

4 There is. It's an elastic band filled with liquid metal which is placed around the penis. Resistance is measured as the electric circuit expands and contracts.

I press the intercom button.

'Yes, all good.'

'Have you inserted the probe?'

'Haha…Yes.'

'Great. I'll just check your pupils are still lined up…could you move slightly to the right again…yep that's perfect. OK. I'll play the images now. There will be a few prompts in between the clips and if you could just use the mouse to respond to those…'

Soothing clouds float across blue skies in front of my eyes. I settle back.

The screen abruptly flicks to a yellowish bedroom. A blonde woman is lying on the floor masturbating, next to some discarded headphones and a haphazard pile of magazines. She is being somewhat vocal about pleasuring herself. Yet I feel anxious about the acoustic guitar at the periphery of the scene, which is leaning very precariously against a window.

Adopting my stomach-crunch position to try and keep my head aligned with the camera, I think, 'I challenge anyone to actually feel aroused in this situation.'

After what seems like several interminable minutes, the screen goes black and a question appears.

'How likely would you be to date this person?'

What the actual fuck?

I consider how likely I would be to date a heterosexual porn actress roughly half my age. I imagine this would be very unlikely indeed. However, I'm feeling generous. I give her a five out of ten.

Then the screen switches to a calming image of what looks like the African savanna. This must be the control clip to return me to a 'normal' arousal state. I hear a familiar voice, which immediately transports me back to the innocence of my nerdy nature-loving childhood.

'As the seasons change and the rain comes, the grasses spring up once again.'

Bloody hell…It's David Attenborough in the sex lab.

Before I get too engrossed in the fast-motion shots of greenery emerging from the desert plains, my visual panorama alters. This time, a man is lying back on a leather sofa fondling his erect penis. 'At least that's a wipeable surface,' I think.

Mind you, there's something about this man with his dark, playful eyes and firm stomach that connects with me. Curious, I lean in a little.

Seeing a naked man feels like a novelty. I can't think when it was…it must have been that time…well, anyway, it's been a long time.

The clip gets cut off just as he was getting really into it. I can't help but feel a little disappointed.

'How likely would you be to date this person?'

This is complicated. I actually felt more interested in looking at him because I could see his face and he was looking at the camera. And yet I'm a lesbian. So surely I would be less likely to go out with a man. I don't want to get caught out and be ejected from the experiment. What if they think I'm a rogue heterosexual women masquerading as a lesbian? Quite what any forty-something straight woman would be doing bunking off work and pretending to be gay just to get paid ninety pounds for watching dimly lit erotica in physically uncomfortable conditions I don't know. I can get paid double that for standing on stage being funny for twenty minutes. This weird procedure already feels like it is taking hours, not helped by my procrastination. I give him four out of ten, one point less than the woman.

During the next David Attenborough clip, I fleetingly remember a chapter from the book *What Do Women Want?* The author, *New York Times* journalist Daniel Bergner, interviews a female scientist who has conducted similar experiments over a number of years with largely heterosexual participants. Where men tend to have a strong correlation between what they *are* physically turned on by and what they *say* they're turned on by, women often have a complete disconnect between the two. Decades of social conditioning prompt us to judge ourselves, play down our private animal instincts and assume that our arousal must surely be narrowly aligned with our publicly stated sexual preferences. I have just done exactly that.

However, Luke's hypothesis, laid out in the *Diva* article I read, is that lesbians have a more 'masculine' specificity of desire. He is anticipating that I will be turned on by women and women alone. Yet as the images unendingly alternate between women and men, on a bed, on a chair, leaning against a wall or kneeling on a tasteful rug, I feel equally intrigued by all of it.

Finally the clips are over. I feel exhausted.

'That's the end of this part of the experiment. If you could carefully remove the probe, put it in the plastic bag and come back out when you're ready, there's a short questionnaire to fill in.'

'OK.'

I go into the larger room to answer some questions about topics including depression, my views on my gender identity and memories of childhood. I can't quite concentrate after the bizarre and slightly sullying experience in the booth. At least it's multiple choice. You can always just guess at those.

'I've finished.'

'Great. The next thing we need to do is scan both of your hands.'

'Ooh. That's interesting. I've heard something about finger lengths being related to sexual orientation. But I wasn't sure if it was just a myth.'

'Well, the theory is that greater exposure to testosterone in the womb generally results in an extreme difference between the lengths of the ring and index fingers. Sometimes the ring finger is as long as the middle finger. And often those women with long ring fingers define as lesbian.'

I inspect my own hands. My ring and index fingers are identical lengths. Yet another way in which I am a 'bad' lesbian.

'When we emailed to book the appointment, you mentioned that I could take a look at my…erm…results.'

'Yes, that's fine. We can take a look at your arousal graphs right now. I haven't analysed it in detail yet of course. But we'll be able to see a general pattern.'

Luke opens up a graph on his computer. The waveform looks tiny, my fluctuations in excitement barely registering on the scale.

'We'll just zoom in a bit…. oh yes, look… This bit corresponds to the first clip of a woman…and this peak here corresponds to…probably another one of the women…she's been very popular…oh that's actually one of the men haha…'

'I quite liked him!'

'You did! Although on average I think the arousal is just slightly higher during the female clips.'

'…and what about during David Attenborough?'

'Haha, oh we don't measure during the control clip.'

'Oh that's a shame.'

'I recorded this data with a pair of twins, both lesbians,' Luke proffers, opening up more graphs.

I gulp slightly as I observe the Himalayan peaks of desire achieved by this horny duo. This is quite different to my feeble undulations. No need to zoom in now.

'This was during the clip of the woman on the bed,' says Luke, almost proudly indicating a particular high.

'Oh right, yes…how old were these twins?'

'Twenty-six.'

Fair enough. When I was in my twenties, I was probably on a much shorter sexual fuse, readier to rapidly get hot and bothered at raunchy images.

The more interesting point is that the younger women's results really do support Luke's hypothesis. There really is a marked difference between the response to watching either women or men.

I have long suspected that I am a little bit bisexual. I prefer my long-term deep, committed, emotional relationships to be with women. And because of that I feel that 'lesbian' has always been the most honest label for me to adopt. But in terms of short-term sexual desires, I think I might be a bit more fluid than a lot of my 'gold star lesbian'[5] friends. Taking part in this strange experiment has helped me come to terms with that.

When I get home, I say to Girlfriend, 'I think I'm a bit turned on by cock.'

'Yeah, me too.'

'I mean not a real cock with an actual man attached…just a hypothetical one…just a pretend one.'

'Haha, it's all good, baby. We both had boyfriends.'

In that moment, I realise that Girlfriend is a keeper. She just gets it…and gets me.

In the old days, I'd have whisked her off to bed. But I have a flashback to the sticky lube and the techno tampon gathering dust in the crotch of my knickers. I head for the shower.

---

5   A lesbian who has never slept with a man.

2

The Lexicon of Breakups

2 years 9 months 2 weeks A.G. (After Girlfriend)

'Would we call ourselves gay or bisexual do you think?'

'Why do you ask?'

'…because I'm going to do the sex lab experiment next week. Y'know, the one I told you about. They want participants who define as lesbian.'

'Well, you do.'

'I know. But it's not that simple, is it? If you say you're a lesbian, people assume you want to sleep with *all* women.'

'Oh god, yes…men think that! I say to them, "Does that mean that, as a straight man, you want to sleep with all women?" and they say, "…Yes!"'

'Ha, that's funny.'

'I'd better stop saying funny things.'

'Why?'

'…because you'll use them in your book.'

'But you'll come across really well if you're funny.'

'Don't give me an "if"! I *am* funny.'

'Anyway, you avoided my question…would you call yourself gay or bisexual?'

'I don't know if I'd use either word really. I know I would never go out with a man again.'

'Why?'

'Because they do my head in.'

'Haha.'

'But the sex was OK. It's not about the sexual side for me, though.'

'It's about an emotional connection?'

'Yes, but I don't think that makes me not a sexual person.'

'I think I'm a demisexual homoromantic.'

'So…you're romantically attracted to women?'

'Yes, and then only sexually attracted when I'm in love.'

'You'll be rubbish in the sex lab then.'

Language is complicated.[1] Even Girlfriend and I, in by far the most emotionally articulate relationship either of us has ever had, struggle to package our desires into neat definitions. How can we begin to discuss the complexity of something as impenetrable as love with mere words? Perhaps that's why we invented our own peculiar form of Morse code. Our 'tap tap tap' signal differentiates our 'I love you' from the ones that we might previously have uttered to other people. Somehow it makes sense to us.

Meanwhile, an equally mysterious, yet rather more contagious, code permeates the contemporary dating community. If I were ever plunged back into the lonely maelstrom of endless swiping, I would have to navigate an unprecedented set of increasingly common behaviours that make Secretive Ex-Girlfriend's breakup email missive look positively quaint. Apps like Tinder have facilitated all kinds of weirdly curt endings. And what's even more befuddling is that there's a whole newfangled language to describe all the modern ways you can now let someone know that you're just not that into them.

Have you ever 'ghosted' anyone? This term started trending in 2014 when comedy writer Hannah VanderPoel turned a 1990s Coolio hit into viral video 'Ghoster's Paradise'. But if you haven't heard of ghosting yet, it means cutting off contact with a love interest without warning or explanation and just…disappearing. An early celebrity example was when Charlize Theron shared with the media that she stopped dating Sean Penn by ignoring his calls.[2]

---

1   I know. I already said that about sex. But language is even *more* complicated.

2   I've never been ghosted romantically. But I have in my professional life. In 2012, I opened for a high-profile comedian at a gig in Whitstable. My set went down well and, in the green room afterwards, this comedian asked me to support him on his forthcoming tour. He gave me his number so I texted him later on my way home…and I never heard from him again. When I checked the number with the promoter, he explained that this comedian was going through a breakup and that might be why he was behaving strangely and not replying. This begs an interesting question…to what extent is a breakup a legitimate excuse for being unreliable?

Ghosting spinoffs include a friendlier alternative, 'caspering', where you do let them down gently before disappearing. Or there's 'submarining', where you suddenly decide to resurface a little while later, perhaps attempting to break the ice with something random like a gif of a baby sloth. Then there's 'orbiting', also sometimes known as 'haunting', where you screen out their calls but continue to view and like their social media posts and photos. This was first defined in a 2018 article on the *Man Repeller* website as keeping someone in your orbit, 'close enough to see each other, but far enough to never talk.' And in a nod to Dickens, 'Marley-ing' is when you suddenly get in touch with your ex out of the blue at Christmas.

Also new to the dating lexicon is 'breadcrumbing': leading someone on with hot flirty messages then going cold at the possibility of meeting up and connecting in the real world.

Then there's 'icing': putting a relationship on hold but keeping it as a reserve option in case nothing better comes along.

That sounds a lot like 'cushioning': keeping someone on the backburner. 'Benching' is a sporting analogy for a similar behaviour: going out playing the field while keeping your date sitting on the sidelines.

And what about 'pocketing', sometimes also known as 'stashing'? Keeping a paramour hidden from friends and family because you're not committed enough to bring them out into the open. Or 'curving', a particularly ambiguous behaviour which relationship coach Ben Edwards says is less 'malicious' than breadcrumbing. Curvers don't knowingly give out crumbs of hope. In fact, curvers never initiate any contact at all. But they do respond to messages. So it sits somewhere between breadcrumbing and ghosting…Toasting, maybe???

Although many of my forty-something friends say, 'Can we get a glossary please?' when I post on Facebook about these myriad bizarre phrases, younger generations find them depressingly familiar. Author and podcaster Dolly Alderton says, 'When I ask an audience of women between the ages of eighteen and thirty how many of them have been ghosted, all the hands shoot up.' She thinks that the prevalence of abruptly vanishing millennial Romeos is 'Something to do with a general feeling of detachment we have from each other. People who are over forty find it extraordinary.'

Yet my 55-year-old friend, comedian and psychotherapist Liz Bentley, thinks that a similar type of avoidant behaviour always existed, despite the lack of a trendy buzzword to describe it. 'When I moved to London I had no phone,' she laughs, acknowledging how odd that seems now. 'You'd meet someone and you'd say, "I fancy you. You fancy me. Let's meet next week at The World's End." And if that person didn't turn up, that was the end of that.' I once took this old-school style of ghosting even further and ripped the page out of my *London A–Z* that included the street where my former love interest resided. This backfired and just meant that I kept getting lost in Archway.

Historian Sally Holloway tells me that, throughout the ages, 'Even without these dedicated terms, men and women still fell out of love, deserted one another, vanished and jilted their partners at the altar.' She explains, 'Some people tried to get around this by going through a person's family and friends to reproach their behaviour and cast doubt on their reputation.' In fact, up until the early twentieth century, a man could be subject to litigation for damages if he committed a 'breach of promise' by going back on an offer of marriage. 'However,' Sally continues, 'in many ways it was easy to disappear as people could just ignore letters sent by unwanted lovers. Some soldiers and sailors returned from war only to discover that the sweethearts they had been writing to had married someone else while they were gone.'

Even if poor dating etiquette is nothing new, I do wonder if giving these practices fun, cutesy names legitimises them. Senior Lecturer in English Literature at the University of Bristol Lesel Dawson says, 'I think naming has an impact on how behaviour is perceived and can also make certain kinds of behaviour more visible.' Meanwhile writer Abigail Tarttelin reckons that these new words 'usualise a lack of courage', and my comedian pal Paul Kerensa thinks that they might 'give people ideas' about how we *should* act in order to look cool. 'Yeah man, I just ghosted her,' we'll say casually, as if merely playing a game populated by utterly disposable fellow players. When we talk online, the other person is reduced to an avatar. In the absence of the oxytocin hit typically triggered by real-life interaction with someone we fancy, we just don't really care.

Yet it seems that there's a huge difference between how we treat others and how we might like to be treated ourselves. Comedian Aziz Ansari conducted a survey for his book *Modern Romance* and found that

73 per cent of a group of young adults, the majority of whom had already confessed to dumping people by text and social media, admitted that they would be upset if someone broke up with them that way. Author of *The Curious History of Dating* Nichi Hodgson says, 'We're in a bit of a liminal stage at the minute where we have this technology but we haven't developed the code of conduct yet to best use it.' There's even a company in Toronto that will send a breakup email or text on your behalf...or if you pay slightly more, create a customised letter or make an awkward phone call. The Breakup Shop was launched by two brothers in 2015 after one of them had been ghosted and thought that even an impersonal businesslike message via a stranger might be preferable to silence.

And where might all this breadcrumbing and curving lead? In my most recent Edinburgh show I emerged onstage in the guise of an armour-clad[3] ghost from the year 2060 to issue a warning that 'love really *is* a battlefield.'[4] A bleak projected timeline of breakups travelled from 'emails, texts and tweets' to 'telepathy' and, finally, 'simply vaporising' the other person. In my dystopian future, dating had become the ultimate blood sport.

Maybe this modern era of seemingly endless dating options being just a click away is turning us all into commitment-phobes. Are we fearful of choosing just one with whom to board the 'relationship escalator'? That's a term for the series of societally recognised stages, from courtship to living together, marriage and kids, that our romances should rapidly and chronologically move through in order to appear 'successful'. Culturally we celebrate longstanding relationships in an ascending hierarchy of wedding anniversary gifts, from lowly paper, leather and wood through tin and lace to sapphire, gold and diamond. The longer you have been together, the better you have done at love. No pressure then. Comedian and activist Kate Smurthwaite says, 'A relationship staircase I could understand...because you'd be choosing to climb up it. But an escalator would be pushing you somewhere without you having any control.'

Whether we actively select it or somehow stumble there nudged along by peer pressure, growing old and grey together does still seem to be held up as the ultimate goal and pinnacle of validation. So does

---

3 Children's toy sword and shield play kit from the Pound Shop. Bargain.
4 Referencing a Pat Benatar song from my childhood to acknowledge the strangely cyclical nature of time. Even as we move forwards, we harvest from the past.

that mean we view a breakup as a 'failure'? Academic and sex and relationships therapist Meg-John Barker is the author of the brilliantly empathetic book *Rewriting The Rules*. Meg-John identifies as non-binary and uses the pronoun 'they'. So it's perhaps no surprise that they are all for questioning some of the traditional language around love. 'Think about the language surrounding breakups,' they say. 'The relationship is *broken*. We have *split* and *separated* from someone. It is *ended* and everything suggests finality, something that is *over* and relegated to the past.' Even 'divorce' comes from the Latin '*di*', meaning apart, and '*vertere*', to turn different ways.

Perhaps that's why some celebrity couples have used a very different vocabulary in order to allow for the possibility of ongoing contact. Gwyneth Paltrow and Chris Martin attracted wide-scale derision in 2014 when they announced their 'conscious uncoupling'. Wasn't it just a hippy-dippy euphemism, an unbearably pretentious way of dressing up a plain old separation? However, over subsequent years they have maintained a healthy friendship, even meeting one another's new partners. Paltrow has said in many interviews that Martin is like a 'brother' to her. Although the phrase 'conscious uncoupling' is forever associated with Gwyneth, it was originally devised by author and family therapist Katherine Woodward Thomas.

And what about Katy Perry and Orlando Bloom? They pressed pause on their liaison in March 2017 by announcing that they were 'taking respectful, loving space'. We all assumed it was curtains for their coupling. However, they rekindled the romance months later and got engaged on Valentine's Day 2019.

Mind you, retaining close ties with an ex could have a more sinister side if it's something you're keeping secret from a current partner. A recent *Refinery29* article pondered whether the strange custom of having a 'breakup-iversary' date might constitute 'micro-cheating'. Micro-cheating is a relatively recent addition to the dating lexicon. In a 2018 *Daily Mail* article, Australian psychologist Melanie Schilling defined it as 'a series of seemingly small actions that indicate a person is emotionally or physically focussed on someone outside of the relationship.' So that might include 'secretly connecting on social media, sharing private jokes, downplaying the seriousness of your relationship to your partner or entering their name in your phone under a code.' Largely speaking, though, I'm of the Gwyneth school of thought. Maintaining some kind of conscious closeness with significant former loves, especially if there are children or animals involved, is often healthy. My friendships with several past partners are testament to that.

Finally, as a salve to heal from our wounds incurred on the battlefield of modern dating, let's think about another word...attachment. Anthropologist Helen Fisher defines the progression of a relationship in three distinct, but interconnected, stages...lust, romantic love and attachment. Many of us now mistake this final stage as 'falling out of love', the intoxicating sexy rollercoaster of novelty replaced by a calmer sense of familiarity and companionship. But it is still *love*.

And it is perhaps in recognition of this fact that love and sex are simultaneously both separate and confusingly muddled that Girlfriend made up her greatest wordplay of all. A few weeks in, she gazed into my eyes and said, 'I love fucking you...and I fucking love you.'

3

I Thought I'd been Ghosted but He'd Just Gone to Prison

Breakup Stories: Louise Leigh

'I was very drunk and wearing what was essentially a nightie. That was the fashion in 1997…I was recovering from a breakup and needed a young, well-endowed and silly man with tattoos to cheer me up. He was all of those things.'

The great thing about presenting a podcast about other people's relationship endings is that I am occasionally forced to stop dwelling on my own past romantic misfortunes. What I'm hoping to do is to learn the secrets of commitment, to work out how to future-proof my connection with Girlfriend. By compiling an exhaustive list of all the possible mistakes and bad choices that my comedy friends have ever made, I will finally know what not to do…and surely, by default, what *to* do. After all, if one group of people have become adept at learning from catastrophe it is comedians. The worst onstage deaths are the performances that enlighten us the most about how to improve. So surely this 'fail better' logic can be applied to love.

I'm in the midst of a chat with standup and writer Louise Leigh. She met Martin while clubbing after a Christmas party, took him back to her place and he just…stayed. After an 'extremely dirty weekend' he sent flowers to her open-plan office with a note saying, 'Bet you're embarrassed now.' He worked in the City and had 'nice ties'. However, he got fired 'for being caught with cocaine...'

'I lived with my mate Larissa and she started to grumble about us both always being there, lolling about on the sofa. And I wanted to fart and not constantly shave. So, after a few weeks, I asked him to spend nights elsewhere. He said he couldn't go back to his boat at Limehouse because it was too cold. So he was going to Big Martin's house, whoever that was.'

It was around that time that she and Larissa realised that the phone was making a weird clicking noise. When they spoke to the police about it, the officers seemed to already know. They wondered if they were being bugged...and why?

After Louise had to have some surgery and her mum came to help her recuperate, she was 'really really ready for Martin to go away.'

And then he did.

'I didn't hear from him while my mum was there. Fine. Then it was Valentine's Day and I didn't hear from him then either, which seemed odd. I still had a lot of his clothes including some horrific faux snakeskin trousers. I had to move out a few months after that so I just took his things to the charity shop and forgot about him. Then one day Larissa came into my work with a handwritten letter she'd received...from Martin, in Pentonville.'

'Sorry to just bugger off but I'm in prison. Please tell Louise I'm really sorry.'

'I was relieved to find out that he wasn't dead and kind of pleased that he hadn't just ghosted me...but had very much moved on by then. I sent Martin a card anyway...one with a Keith Haring picture of a man in a clock saying, "Sorry to hear you're doing time" and didn't think about him again.'

Until Martin contacted her on Facebook ten years later...

'He said he often thought of me very fondly. I replied saying, "That's nice. I'm married with kids."'

Louise's takeaway from this story was that, although Martin wasn't 'the one', she did want to be with somebody fun and spontaneous as opposed to her previous, more staid, partner.

It's interesting how we steer towards or away from particular character traits based on our previous relationship experiences. It stung that my two brief brushes with infidelity came back to back. Because I really thought that Secretive Ex-Girlfriend seemed solid, kind and reliable in comparison to Agoraphobic Ex-Girlfriend. But Agoraphobic Ex-Girlfriend was just so 'out there' as a partner choice that almost anyone would have seemed relatively reliable. During those lonely, wilderness years, I made the mistake of attaching a higher importance to physical attraction than to the solid basis of friendship that I'd had with Boozy Ex-Girlfriend and eventually returned to with Nice Ex-Girlfriend. And then with Girlfriend both things seemed to converge. Finally! Hooray!

Romantic love is a bit like a video game where we are constantly unlocking levels, sometimes dropping back a stage when we make a bad choice. Or perhaps it's like spinning plates. As soon as one thing is sorted, another thing crashes to the floor.

My takeaway from this story is that Louise is a much better judge than I of the difference between what should be a long-term romantic prospect and what should only constitute a short-term one.

Although Martin conveniently 'buggered off' to prison, Louise was all ready to break things off anyway. Martin had served his purpose as a little light relief after her more serious breakup. Whereas, with both Secretive Ex-Girlfriend[1] and Agoraphobic Ex-Girlfriend, I fell headlong into a trap of outstaying the optimum duration of a fun fling. Once you stick around past the six-month mark, you start believing that you just need to change your unreliable partner a little bit so that you can settle down together. Then after a year or two, it's even harder to leave. It feels foolish to tolerate something uncomfortable for so long unless you somehow change it, turn it around over time. So this fictional, impossible 'victory' becomes as tantalising as a mirage in the desert. 'If I stay a bit longer, she's going to come out', 'If I stay a bit longer, she's going to overcome her anxiety'…and *then* we will be happy and get married, just like in the movies.

One way or another, the compelling societal script attached to love has a spooky way of pressuring you onto the relationship escalator…and then dashing your hopes if it's not a thrilling upwards lifelong journey full of fireworks, passion, fulfilment and fun. But anyone who travels regularly on a city underground or subway system will know that escalators frequently break down and require maintenance.

---

1 Goddammit, why couldn't she just have committed a crime and got herself locked up? That might've been easier.

4

Great Expectations

2 years 8 months A.G. (After Girlfriend)

'So we're just like all those other couples now.'

'What do you mean?…A bit boring?'

Conversations like this make me nervous. Last time my sense of adventure was questioned, we were on a cycle track at Bedgebury Forest. I went hurtling downhill at top speed just to prove a point…and fell off.

'Yeah. We don't go out at weekends. I work hard and live for the weekend. But then it comes around and we don't do anything.'

'We do go out. It's just that we do things that revolve around places we can take the dog. So I guess we're just like all those other couples that have a dog…or a child.'

We are having lunch in a pub. It is Saturday. So technically we are out at the weekend. But I know what Girlfriend means. Although the setting might be idyllic, with Dog curled up in front of a roaring fire, we are in muddy jeans and wellies rather than sexy party clothes and makeup. We aren't chatting and laughing with other people. We aren't at the cinema, theatre or a fancy event. The highlight of our morning has been spotting a signpost pointing to a 'moated manor'…which turned out to be a sunken ruined chimney in the middle of a pond.

This conversation highlights the fundamental difference in our psychologies. She wants things to be fun. I want things to be meaningful. I don't mind being boring sometimes if I'm doing it with the right person. She is an example of Freud's 'pleasure principle' and I lean more towards the ideas of Austrian psychiatrist Viktor Frankl and his 'logotherapy'. She wants to socialise. Meanwhile I'm conserving energy for my next creative quest. In a few months or so, we will arrive back on the same page. I will need to socialise again because I'll have a creative quest to tell people about.

We are both a complex mix of introvert and extrovert. I have a seemingly outgoing job. Yet comedy is the perfect introvert's disguise. You can fool a room into thinking you are confident because you have a microphone and an armoury of funny things to say. Many times I've had disappointed admirers say, 'Oh I thought you'd be like you are onstage,' when we spend time together in real life. Whereas Girlfriend can put on a good show of small talk when required but goes to pieces at the thought of speaking in public.

But these qualities are only relevant relative to the people you're surrounded by. When I went out with Secretive Ex-Girlfriend and Agoraphobic Ex-Girlfriend, they were both, arguably, more introverted than me. Suddenly I was the gregarious one, the leader, the decision-maker. I felt empowered by my new role. It was brilliant. Yet all along, each resented the dynamic that had been established and plotted my ultimate destabilising demise. I have been fearful of taking charge ever since.

A man walks over to our table alongside a cherubic toddler.

'Is it OK for him to say hello to the dog?'

'Yes, of course. She'll love it.'

Dog rolls onto her back obligingly and wags her tail at being clumsily patted all over.

The man asks all about Dog, her breed, her age, her behaviour and the effectiveness of the tracking device we have clipped to her collar. He seems quite taken with her. I wonder if we are supposed to ask similar questions about his son. What is the etiquette?

'Will you get one?' asks Girlfriend.

'Not at the moment. My wife doesn't like dogs.'

I look across to the woman sitting alone at their table and wonder how long it'll be before she's chasing a rampant puppy around the house trying to retrieve half-chewed knickers from its jaws.

A long-term relationship is all about compromise, a partner trampling all over the boundaries and fantasies we had carefully constructed during our carefree single days. Valentine's cards and love songs don't alert us to this. The narratives about romance that the mass media present us with during our adolescence don't inform or prepare us in any way for the mind-numbing cycle of negotiation and conciliation that is to come. There is no public health warning about the 'expectation gap', the yawning chasm of dissonance that lies between how we are told that love plays out and how it actually does.

Psychotherapist and former *Diva* magazine editor Jane Czyzselska says, 'Popular white cis-heteronormative culture teaches us a whole bunch of stuff that isn't particularly helpful…the idea that there's "the one", that it's something that happens between two people only, that it exists as a precursor to sex or as part of the lead-up to sex, that romance will make you happy, that romance is red hearts, flowers and chocolates, that there's an expected course of events with one stage leading to the next stage, that one person (and if it's heterosexual, the man) leads the process and that it's unconventional if the woman is to do so.'

As a teenager, I wanted to be Bruce Willis' character David in the television show *Moonlighting*. I adored the unpredictable 'will they won't they' frisson between him and Cybill Shepherd's Maddie. So perhaps it's no surprise that for years I was drawn to people who were mercurial, elusive and impossible to pin down. A reliable, caring partner feels alien to me.

Comedian Sajeela Kershi was addicted to Mills & Boon romance novels and traded them in the school playground 'like it was a drug deal'. The narrative template of these books was 'man pursues woman, woman says no, man pursues woman again and again until she gives in'. Sajeela then said 'Yes' to a man who relentlessly pursued her because she had learned that this was a demonstration of 'true love'. 'No wonder I never made a relationship work,' she laughs.

The nineties equivalent was the *Point Romance* book series. Author and filmmaker Nat Luurtsema was a fan. 'The protagonist was always a beautiful perky blonde girl and her boyfriend was always really handsome but moody. She would look after him. So I dated a succession of quite difficult men.'

Katy Brand's favourite films were *Dirty Dancing*, *Mary Poppins* and *The Sound of Music* because they all featured 'a strident bossy woman coming into people's lives uninvited and trying to sort them out.' She says, 'I think that's still my model for relationships. Luckily I have a very adaptable husband who indulges me and lets me sort things out.'

Meanwhile Richard Herring looked to his parents for an example of how love ought to be: 'They have been together since they were thirteen. When I was a teenager, I thought that's what would happen to me as well. So when I had my first girlfriend and that went wrong, it kind of blew everything apart really.'

But although he then spent many years falling for people who would treat him 'quite badly' and where he often 'wasn't a great boyfriend' he feels that those relationships taught him more than the eventual good ones. So he ponders whether it's actually romantic after all to hook up with the first person you meet 'if you've got nothing to compare it to. Or is it more romantic to go out with 500 people and then say, "You were the best one. Congratulations, you've won the competition. Let's get married"?'

Author and co-founder of *The Quietus* music website, Luke Turner, thinks, 'You're much better off fucking up all your relationships until you're about forty. You have a different understanding. The more failed relationships you've had, the better your future ones are going to be. You've worked out how to negotiate and compromise. Being in love isn't always exciting. It's about tolerance and having a laugh. That's the recipe for success and you only realise that later in life.' This is something that I've come to think of as the 'forty love' rule. Only at midlife do we start to figure out what we actually want, as opposed to what we think we do.

Professor Jacqui Gabb of The Open University's *Enduring Love* project has spent years documenting what helps people to sustain relationships. She says that the ideal of 'the one' perfect partner who will be everything to us is such an unrealistic goal that, 'Many people who aspire to it are often unhappy when the reality of life doesn't match up to this fantasy. Some people who buy into this dream end up bouncing from one partner to another as they try to find the non-existent person who has no flaws or shortcomings. Others stay in relationships that aren't good for them because they fear the stigma of being single or because they convince themselves that this person is "the one", so they have to stick with them whatever.'

As I ponder Jacqui's wise words, I think about my friends, Angie and Liz, and the heightened addictive drama of their on-off four-year rollercoaster affair.

Liz and I first met in the 1990s. A queue of disparate female musicians, some holding instruments, snaked around the dusty stairs at a West London fringe pub theatre. Waiting to audition for a play about a girl band, I struck up conversation with the skinny and gregarious dark-haired drummer behind me. I knew we were going to be allies forever, regardless of whether we were chosen for the cast.[1] What neither of us knew then was that she was bipolar. Over the years, it gets harder to rely on someone when they can't quite rely on themselves. The timeline of our friendship contains a decade-long gap. Liz just disappeared and became something of a mythical figure in my social circle. Had anyone seen her? Did anyone know where she was or what she was doing? And then she was back, an all-too-familiar cackle cutting across the chatter in the pub function room where I was due to perform, causing me to do a double-take, a 360-degree turn right there on the spot. It couldn't be…Or could it? It was! We bounced up and down in joy for what seemed like a full minute, 40-year-old women behaving like children on pogo sticks as if all the ravages of adulthood hadn't altered them at all.

A year or two later, I bonded with vulnerable, warm-hearted singleton Angie on a dating site over our shared love of comedy. Despite meeting online, it was clear from the outset that the dynamic of our chat was not flirtatious. She started coming to my gigs with friends, her booming, supportive laugh a reassuring sound in the less friendly rooms. We compared notes about our colourful relationship histories at lunch dates in town, often when I was en route to see my therapist, an easy silliness punctuating our collective sadness.

Ever since I introduced them at my birthday party and they began a relationship, things within our friendship group have been dramatic.[2] They are often on opposite sides of the room in the audience at my podcast recordings, crying after yet another row. Tellingly, they call themselves, 'the Liz Taylor and Richard Burton of the lesbian world.' Sometimes two people might desire and need each other with all the intensity and fire of a shooting star. But is that enough? Perhaps our human attachments

---

1 We weren't.
2 It's tough for me to be around this drama…mostly because I don't like seeing my friends hurting so badly. But also because the addict part of me misses that drama. It's a bit like being a former alcoholic surrounded by people who are still drinking. If you're a former love addict looking to settle into a long-term relationship, it helps if your friends do the same.

need to be rather more prosaic if they are to survive...and if we are to survive them.

Danish comedian Sofie Hagen says that she went from thinking that relationships full of conflict were 'romantic' because they seemed to happen 'on a bridge in the rain, screaming' to a realisation that 'maybe love is just meant to be nice.' Author and journalist Nichi Hodgson comes from a family of multiple divorces, so is particularly interested in what makes commitment work. She dispels soulmate myths, explaining, 'If the partnership matters to you above all else, there's probably any number of people you can make it work with.'

Dr Anna Machin is an evolutionary anthropologist who has studied human relationships for many years. She first came to my attention as part of an expert panel on the TV show *Married at First Sight*. She says, 'We get obsessed with our Western view of what love is. We see it as this "happy, skipping along through the daisies" emotion. Whereas if you ask people around the world, particularly among the older generation in China, they will describe it as quite a negative state, associated with compromise, frustration and sacrifice...which is perhaps more realistic.' In India, science communicator Charvy Narain tells me, 'Traditionally, commitment is about two families marrying. There's a lot more emphasis on female kinship and your relationship with your sister-in-law or songs you sing with your mother-in-law. The weight of your love isn't just on one person.'

Comedian and podcaster Caroline Mabey reckons that 'The key to staying together is tolerating mediocrity. After you have a child, it becomes more like a business. The way we get through is by channelling kindness, by mining for infinite patience.' Jacqui Gabb conducted a research study with more than 5,000 people in long-term relationships and found that everyday thoughtful acts such as bringing a partner a cup of tea or breakfast in bed were a far more crucial 'glue' holding things together than lavish gifts or sexual passion. Although these gestures varied around the world – from 'packing an intricate lunchbox in Japan', to 'warming up the car on a cold morning in Canada' or 'going out in the rain to buy bread rolls in Germany' – the principle is the same. If you're nice to each other, you might avoid a breakup.

And it seems that, although it's a desperately tedious struggle, many of us still want to stay together for as long as we can. Says

Richard Herring, 'When you have the strength of a loving family, the rewards are few but still better than what you'd get from a new person. A long-term relationship is more difficult *and* more satisfying than falling in love with different people and staying with each of them for six months.'

And yet the revolving door of rapid serial monogamy is something very familiar to me...

5

Stuck in the Middle

2 years 7 months A.G. (After Girlfriend)

'I can't understand why she's so shocked I broke up with her. I kept telling her I was unhappy for the entire three years.'

'Maybe she's surprised that you suddenly did something about it.'

Girlfriend is advising our friend Becky, a fiercely intelligent and opinionated, slightly dishevelled astrophysicist and musician, about her recent separation with Lena, a self-deprecating Austrian comedian with a charmingly terrible grasp of the English language. Although we are perhaps slightly closer to Becky, I have known Lena via the comedy circuit for much longer.

I'm impressed by Girlfriend's insight. While it's true that Becky regularly moaned to anyone who would listen about Lena's ongoing friendship with her recent ex, we assumed that they would stay together. They were a super-fun, seemingly well-matched couple, with similarly chaotic, studenty approaches to life, booze and partying.

Being friends with another couple helped to solidify my bond with Girlfriend. It meant that we existed outside of our own domestic bubble, out in the world. Their combined haphazard sensibilities livened and loosened us up a bit. And we probably need a bit of that sometimes.

So, while of course I wouldn't want Becky to remain in a situation that is miserable for her, there's a little part of me that is disappointed. I've spent all afternoon cooking a heartache-soothing vegan chilli, thinking that Lena was probably the one that did the dumping…when, in actual fact, Becky is the one who has called time on our fun foursome.

It's strange how we think of endings in such binary terms – of good and bad, blameless dumpees and heartless dumpers, heroes and villains. My instinct is always to feel hurt by the active party, the sender of the breakup missive, and feel empathy for the one in shock, the recipient. It's easy when it's a straight pal who has been cheated on or betrayed in some way by some abstract man. Yet these people are both our friends and I know it's more complicated. Relationship and wellbeing coach Shula Melamed advises caution when committing allegiance to one side or the other, suggesting, 'When you're in a sexual relationship with another person, it can really trigger other parts of your psychological profile – things that as a friend you might not ever witness because you don't trigger that person in the same way that an intimate partner does.' Undoubtedly there are facets of both Becky and Lena that we just don't know. In any breakup, there are always two stories, both emotionally authentic and true in their own way.

Perhaps I'm just feeling a bit disgruntled with Becky because this conversation comes mere days after a longstanding pal messaged to say that she's moved back up North after her wife told her she didn't feel 'that way' any more, Angie and Liz have had yet another brutal argument and Facebook has revealed that a former writing colleague has absconded with her wife's best friend.

All kinds of theories exist as to why queer women separate so frequently. Time and time again, articles about the high lesbian divorce rates in the UK, the Netherlands and other European countries quote old-school gay activists on our tendency to 'U-haul' (in other words, to move in together and commit with ridiculous haste). The assumption seems to be that burning through the early stages of attraction so frenetically means that we will also reach the end of the partnership more quickly. Yet to focus on such lazy stereotypes seems like lousy journalism.

It is true. We do move quickly.

However, the key data to pay attention to here is the fact that the overwhelming majority of heterosexual divorces are initiated by women. Women, of all sexualities, appear to be more likely to leave a relationship. Even in Netflix teen comedy *Sex Education*, it is the young women who are fearless enough to call time on hook-ups that aren't quite working.

When Ola realises that Otis isn't in love with her, she dumps him rather than stay in an uncomfortable situation.

So, of course a relationship between two women is more likely to break down than one between a man and a woman, and more likely still than one between two men. It's just basic maths. The good news for lesbians is that they are more likely to separate amicably and respectfully. Conscious uncoupling, or some form of it, was pioneered by us long before Gwyneth turned it into a global phenomenon.

In my opinion, the reason why all these women are leaving relationships is simple. The structures of commitment, marriage and monogamy within which we conduct our romantic relationships have all been forged in the heteronormative, patriarchal interest. These societal straitjackets are less comfortable for women, lesbians in particular. Sometimes it is the looming oppression of these structures, rather than the actions of our actual partner, that are corrosive to our sense of self. A woman's identity, status and attractiveness are under constant scrutiny and threat. Sometimes that means jettisoning a relationship that might seem 'good on paper' in order to stay whole.

Or sometimes it may just be that our partner turns out to be a dick. And women can't afford to put up with that. Whereas men may not care or notice because they have so much less disadvantage to offset in the first place.

In recent years, literature has emerged arguing that, contrary to decades of Western social conditioning, women are not wired for long-term monogamy. In her book *Untrue*, New York author Wednesday Martin says that women are rapidly 'closing the infidelity gap.' Men may have long felt entitled to sexual novelty yet women may be the ones who have even more of an urgent primal drive towards it. Transfer this restless psychology over to female-female relationships and you'd expect our community to be littered with affairs. However, the preferred script among my peer group seems to be one of rapidly rotating intense serial pairings with an occasional clandestine overlap and a hell of a lot of rebound flings. My friend Kat says, 'When suffering from a broken heart, the most common course of action taken by human beings is to latch onto a similar object of their affection in order to fill the gaping void.'

I wonder if anyone is truly happier in the long run after swapping one partner for another. What happens when the new, exciting person becomes boring? My friend Abigail says, 'Sometimes we all go through stages where we think, "I feel bad about my life and maybe if I changed my partner I'd feel better." But then you realise that's a really bad idea.'

Some women exhaust all options and then end up back with an ex. One Facebook friend did so after a doorstep declaration akin to the *Love Actually* scene where Andrew Lincoln reveals his hitherto undisclosed desire for Keira Knightley via a series of handwritten cue cards. But since all her mates had spent weeks saying, 'Oh yeah, that relationship was never right for you anyway', she felt she had to keep the reunion secret. That proved challenging because, 'You almost shut yourself off from a big part of each other's lives.' So it ended…again.

Although science provides some context to the swirling miasma of serial monogamy, it's still exhausting to stand on this constantly shifting sand. Breaking up and staying together are inextricable. You can't do one without thinking about the other. To be a lesbian in a romantic relationship is like perching anxiously at a cliff's edge looking down to the wild seas of love addiction below…and wondering when you'll be pulled back in. When I'm surrounded by the acrimonious wreckage of my friends' partnerships, I begin to wonder if I'm misguided in my belief that Girlfriend and I will survive. Surely every time someone close to us breaks up, it increases the probability that we will? As the social contagion closes in, I become more reclusive.

Nevertheless I feel an urge to make contact with Lena. But it's tricky. A message will alert her that Becky has already told us about the split and presented her side of the story. I decide to go for it.

'How are you? We heard about you and Becky and were really sad and surprised. Hope to see you sometime soon. We really want to stay friends with both of you. Take care.'

'Was a surprise for me too. All very painful but it is for the best.'

'Yes I'm sorry it's such a shitty time.'

'It is but at least I already managed to write a whole set about it! So if you need another performer for *The Breakup Monologues*…'

Holy fuck. Now there's a dilemma. Should I give one of our friends a platform from which to discuss being dumped by another of our friends?

'Lena is a quirky self-deprecating performer. Her jokes aren't attacks on others, more like a piss-take of her own behaviour,' I reason to myself.

'Sure. How about guesting on my February show?'

Girlfriend is going to kill me. Not to mention Becky.

Maybe I have made a mistake.

But I have to admit I miss Becky and Lena as a couple. I have a genuine affection for each of them. As a result, I'm struggling to think rationally about their breakup even though it isn't really anything to do with me. They only got together a matter of weeks before Girlfriend and I did. So they always felt like a barometer of a relationship stage just slightly ahead of ours. Lesbian relationships are part of such a delicate ecosystem of interconnected friendships that it kicks up the dust for everyone else when two people separate.[1]

And, as far as I could tell, Becky and Lena seemed very happy together when we were all on a skiing holiday just a few months ago...

---

1 My utopia would probably be reincarnation as a female bonobo. Bonobo society is matriarchal. This is largely due to the fact that their physiology makes female-female sex really easy and enjoyable. They have a massive protruding clitoris that they can rub against another massive protruding clitoris. This sounds logistically superior to the awkward physicality of human lesbian sex. Because the female bonobos are having such great sex together, they form bonds and help one another. They almost forget about the males, who meekly pop up now and again to say, 'Errr...Hello!? We are over here! Could we have some sex as well, please?' Decades ago, lesbian feminists tried to live in communes and emulate this sort of utopia. However, humans can't help falling in love and splitting the group into nuclear 'couple' and 'family' units, thus diluting the power of the alliance with betrayals and breakups. However separatist we are, we can't seem to escape patriarchal structures.

6

It's All Downhill from Here

2 years 4 months A.G. (After Girlfriend)

'I hope Lena appreciates just how much of a sign of my love for her this is that I'm putting myself through this.'

'I know what you mean. I guess it'll start off easy though, won't it? What's the time now anyway?'

'It's five past. Maybe he's forgotten about us. Shall we bunk off and just have a hot chocolate and then pretend that we did the lesson?'

'Oh God yes!…Although there's a bloke waving at us over there. Bugger, maybe that's him.'

Becky and I smile sweetly at the stubbly instructor sauntering towards us with skis casually slung over his shoulder.

Girlfriend and Lena swoop into a perfect parallel stop alongside us, having just completed a black run. Routes are coded according to difficulty. Black, with its deathly associations, seems an appropriate descriptor for the vertical cliff face looming in front of us. Next is red. These runs might be slightly less steep but are narrow and tricky to navigate in the long, winding S-shape preferred by the less experienced skier. On the resort map, they trickle like lines of blood down the mountain.

'Hey! Are you checking up on us?'

'Just seeing you off to your lesson before we jump back on the lift up to the top again…'

Girlfriend's effortless superiority at any kind of physical exercise or sport is so annoying. At least this week I have an ally in Becky. She has zero experience, while my ski CV consists of a sole school trip thirty years ago. And we don't have to worry about holding our partners up as they can do the more adventurous runs together. Although it does seem like they've skied the entirety of the modest resort within the first hour or so. Bansko is hardly Val d'Isère in terms of expanse and variety.

Becky and I follow our monosyllabic new leader, gingerly slide-shuffling like clumsy over-dressed penguins, over to the nursery slope button lift.

True to their haphazard form, Lena and Becky have flown to Bulgaria with hand luggage only. Who the hell does that on a ski holiday? Girlfriend, always overprepared, has loaned them spare jackets and sunglasses to save them from freezing and snow-blindness. For once, her packing lists and holiday spreadsheets have come into their own. While I often think that organising the fuck out of something can equate to organising the fun out of it, a ski holiday is different. It's no fun being cold. So I'm grateful for the endless pairs of snug, dry spare socks that emerge from her suitcase like it is Moominmamma's handbag. She has also been the one to arrange care for Dog and Cat while we are away, with her mum Glenda and our neighbour respectively.

As the lesson progresses, my instincts about which way to lean demonstrate that the ancient school trip must still be lodged in my memory somewhere. Just as well, because Instructor is hopeless. Becky is having trouble slowing down and stopping, surely the basic first skill required when one's feet are strapped to two sliding sticks.

'Push, push,' says Instructor, demonstrating a wide snowplough and digging the inside edges of his skis into the crisp surface of the tiny hill.

'I don't know what you mean.'

Nevertheless, we keep getting back on the lift to repeat our tiny descent without any further meaningful feedback about our technique. At least the sky is a glorious blue and a warm winter sun is beating down on the crunchy whiteness below our stuttering feet.

When Girlfriend and Lena collect us at lunchtime, they ask if we are ready to be taken on the chairlift to the top of a short blue run. Blue is the next level up from green, the virtually horizontal piste that we have started on.

Instructor shrugs. Girlfriend and Lena take that as a yes.

'Ski up to the line…wait wait…look behind you.'

The chairlift swings round and slaps our knees from behind, swooping us up in a dishevelled mess.

'Whooo…it suddenly went fast then…bloody hell…can you hold my gloves a minute?…What do I do with my skis now? '

'Let me pull this bar down and then you rest them on that.'

'What do we do about getting off?'

'Don't worry about that just yet.'

'But I am worried.'

'OK. Here we go. I'll lift this up again and just rest your skis flat on the top of that little ramp then let it push you off gently…'

'Now?…er…argh…oh crap.'

I manage to stay upright and ski semi-gracefully off the lift. I look behind and poor Becky is in a heap on the floor, her anxiety trebled as the so-called 'blood wagon', a sledge-stretcher pulled along by a little truck with a siren, hurtles past on a rescue mission.

Girlfriend helps her up and starts skiing backwards an arm's length in front of her.

'I'll stay right here so that you can't get out of control. If you crash, you'll only crash into me and it'll be fine.'

After a calm moment coasting along a flat wide path lined by fir trees, we turn left and a relatively steep descent hovers into view.

Becky freaks out.

'I can't do it. No way. Can I just take my skis off and walk down?'

I think about the ungainliness of the tight ski boots and wonder how long this might take. I'm a bit hungry and have already devoured the emergency Twix in my lift pass pocket. I'm hoping that Girlfriend has a better plan.

'I'm here. It'll be fine. I'll guide you. We'll just take it really slowly… you've got this.'

Becky takes some deliberate breaths and allows her skis to edge forwards.

My heart flutters a little as I see how kind, patient and skilled Girlfriend is. This is the closest I may ever get to watching her do her job. Although she works with tennis players, she could pretty much help anyone in any sport to better fulfil their physical potential. We will get down in one piece thanks to her. In the urgency of this situation, her superior prowess becomes sexy rather than irritating.

'You're doing great, baby,' she calls out to me as I zigzag slightly ahead of them, snowploughing my way down more confidently now to the pretty wooden pizza bar below.

Lena, oblivious to just how much we've had to support Becky through her panic, has sped all the way down there already.

When Girlfriend eventually arrives with a shaky and relieved Becky in tow, she glances at Lena. Nobody else would spot it. But I can tell that look means, 'Where the hell were *you*?'

Sometimes the displacement of being on holiday, away from our normal routines and the distractions of work, shines a spotlight on the tiny fractures in a relationship that may come to haunt us later.

The intensity of being together around the clock accelerates the evolution of the relationship…often in the wrong direction (or perhaps, ultimately, the right direction). There are even some travel insurers who will cover the cost of a call and session with a relationship counsellor while you're away.

In 2009, I travelled to Sydney with Secretive Ex-Girlfriend to do some gigs as part of the Mardi Gras festival. In order to make the month-long trip affordable, we stayed with her ex in her cosy two-bedroom apartment. Julie was warm and down-to-earth, with a mass of dishevelled dark curly hair and a thoughtfully generous selection of English teabags and biscuits. Yet once the initial excitement of arriving, exploring the neighbourhood and getting to know her had subsided, the unresolved dynamic between her and my partner became clearer to me. They stayed up later and later listening to The Whitlams, an Aussie band whose music had clearly been significant during their romantic relationship. I felt so clumsy, sitting there trying to gatecrash their connection, to understand the in-jokes, desperately trying to stay awake and not leave them alone together. And, worse still, I had nowhere to go. We had a week left before heading back to London. There was nobody else in Sydney I could go and stay with. Back then, I didn't have the kind of money to cover a hotel or rebooking a flight.

On the final day, I tried to escape for a while by taking Julie's little dog Mitzi out for a long walk. But Mitzi dug her paws into the pavement and refused to go anywhere. So I sat down alongside her and confided, 'I know I should leave her…but I can't.'

Mitzi yawned, still clinging to the kerb. Then a dramatic Sydney rain shower arrived from nowhere and forced us back into the house, back into the tension.

It was as if, rather than being rational and seeing that my partner was being a dick, I felt more locked in than ever. The threat of romantic and sexual competition fuelled my desire for her. The more primitive animal, or limbic, parts of my brain took over. I was in a hypervigilant panic, policing her every move. I had to win, even if I had to win ugly.

When we were finally on our plane home, we hit some turbulence. I stoically took Secretive Ex-Girlfriend's hand, realising that, in that moment, my fear of a plane crash was substantially less than my fear of her leaving me.

Some of my friends have had similar experiences of being marooned somewhere with a partner they're no longer getting on with. When comedy writer and producer Miles Chapman was in his early twenties, he met a French exchange student called Stephanie through a friend. They hit it off and she asked him to come and stay with her family in France. However, not long after he'd driven off the ferry, she said, 'I don't think we should be together.' He drove her to a party, where she spent most of the evening snogging another bloke. 'They were even leaning against my car!' Miles exclaims. The next day, he set off to get on the first ferry home. But it was peak season and they had nothing available for a week. Miles whiled away the days eating ice cream with Stephanie's younger brother Fabrice. 'I just looked like a paedophile hanging out with this 12-year-old,' he sighs, laughing.

Musician, comedian and broadcaster Faye Treacy hadn't even reached her destination when she received a breakup message from the lover she was on her way to see. Drummer and on-off partner Sam had Facetimed her and invited her out to New York. 'Why don't you come and see me?' he said. Faye recalls that, 'He did go silent the week before but I went to Heathrow anyway and got on a plane.' But then the dreaded text came through: 'I'm really sorry. I actually have a fiancé. I was having a wobble when I contacted you.' Faye decided that the best thing to do was to get hammered on the flight and arrive 'drooling slightly' at JFK airport. She found herself an Airbnb and treated herself to a lovely holiday to ease her feelings of indignation and hurt.

Solo international adventures can, ultimately, be incredibly healing.[1]

When travel writer Anna Hart was a 21-year-old literature student, she decided to get over her ex by going on a ten-day bender in Holland with three of his best friends. Chatting to me on *Radio Diva*,[2] she described it as a 'hedonistic disaster of a heartbreak trip' during which she 'slept on the floor wrapped in a curtain in a drug dealer's attic.' After a few days, however, she realised she needed a holiday from her holiday. She checked herself into a dorm in a hostel and started visiting museums and galleries instead of dark, sticky bars and nightclubs, sensing just how healing and enriching travel can be when you get it right.

Another thing she said which really struck me was that it took her a 'long time to become a good traveller.' It's a simple idea but a pretty good metaphor for travelling through our romantic relationships. Most of us are idiot tourists to begin with, arrogantly assuming that a casual glance at a guide book equips us to know our way around a place. On a recent solo trip to Berlin, I had my most rewarding day walking to the south of the city to a disused Nazi airfield which had been converted into a countercultural ramshackle park full of quirky makeshift art and urban gardens. This park was recommended by a wise, uber-cool woman I met in a sex shop, not by any official tourist literature.

In the same way, we think we know all about love and sex after watching a couple of Hollywood romcoms. We have naive crushes like I did on Older Ex-Girlfriend. We don blinkers and then get upset when obviously incompatible partnerships end in devastating drama. And then we grow up and start to take advice from real people who actually know what they're talking about. We detour through a few more interesting back streets and start to become more resilient to the little bumps in the road that are a standard part of any journey, even one we have carefully chosen and very much want to continue on.

---

1 There's an app called Breakup Tours which helps you plan a cathartic solo trip.
2 LGBTQI magazine show sponsored by *Diva* Magazine and broadcast weekly on anarchic, artsy London station Resonance FM. I presented and produced for three years alongside musician and actor Heather Peace, having previously hosted an award-winning show called *Out in South London* in the same slot. Sadly, as with all the best things in life, the money ran out and we had a farewell Christmas show in December 2019.

7

The Moths of Doom

2 years A.G. (After Girlfriend)

What Does Heartbreak *Feel* Like...and Why?

'I still love you.'

'I know. But you don't like me at the moment, do you?'

We are looking at each other through one eye, the other obscured by nestling into a pillow. Half hiding like this, we are able to be honest. When Girlfriend and I are out of sync, there's a little black hole of anxiety that gnaws away in my stomach, that temporary little fear that maybe we've had our last good day together without even realising, without relishing each final second. I know she feels it too. It's a sensation that Marian Pashley, Pippa Evans and I once discussed on the podcast. Marian called it 'the moths of doom', a sort of inverse to the butterflies of love fluttering around in your tummy when things are good and exciting.

This evening isn't a full-blown moth attack. On a scale of one to five, where one represents a minor disagreement about saucepans and five represents a discovery of a partner's spare phone full of messages from a secret lover, we are currently at a two or three. We are just a bit exhausted and cranky as we near the end of our first year of living together, a year that has been full of disruption. Building works, the arrival of a naughty puppy, adjusting to Girlfriend's obsessive cleanliness and a million micro-negotiations about what to cook for dinner have all taken their toll on me. I've had a recurring heavy cold and chest infection. Getting through gigs with a weakened voice has been a struggle. I just can't seem to get better. I feel a bit under siege. Yet it seems churlish to blame Girlfriend's admirable efforts in finding a home for us.

Maybe it's something to do with the house itself. Perhaps I have sick building syndrome. I've looked it up repeatedly over the past few weeks. Possible symptoms include headaches, blocked nose, dry eyes and tiredness. I have all of those. I must be allergic to the house. This is highly inconvenient. Girlfriend had to survive months of stress trying to sell her old flat. She loves this house and isn't going to move any time soon. I'm just going to have to find a way to fall in love with it too.

So that leaves me looking for another scapegoat for my malaise. And just like that, one pitter-patters into the room on four dirty paws. Dog. Yes, that's it. My health and energy levels have definitely plummeted since she arrived.

Lately I've bumped into a spate of old friends who say things to the effect of, 'Oh once we got a dog, it ruined our relationship/sex life/social life…' And there's suddenly so much washing…dog towels, blankets, and cushions that Dog has been sick on or peed on.

And then there's the extreme dog walks to contend with. Dog is a lethal combination of cocker spaniel and beagle, high energy and terrible recall. Even the fancy tracking gadget that Girlfriend has invested in is not foolproof. One day recently I went crawling through mud and brambles deep into the woods, following the little red icon on the phone app. A small white box flashed at me from the dirt. Dog had managed to unclip it from her collar and merrily continue on her adventures untraced.

'Oh no, she's getting mud everywhere. I thought you said you wiped her paws after you took her out this afternoon?'

'I tried to but she kept biting me…'

'She's just playing. You need to be firmer with her. She might've needed a bath today if she's that filthy.'

'Do you really think we should keep her?'

'What??'

'Well it just feels like it's been very stressful so far having a dog.'

'But I love her! Don't you?'

'Well, yes. I mean, look at her. She's gorgeous. If there was a Tinder for pets, I would choose her based on looks. But she's also a pain in the arse. I'm struggling to cope with her on my own during the day while I'm supposed to be working. When I left her downstairs for ten minutes last week, she chewed up my glasses. I loved those glasses. And they were expensive.'

'Maybe we could get a dog walker to take her out for a bit each day. Would that help?'

'I guess so.'

'Do you want to do it or do I have to sort it out?'

'I think a woman handed me a business card the other day. I'll look for it.'

For now, we are both placated by this potential practical solution. The moths of doom flutter away as Girlfriend mops away Dog's tiny paw prints.

Our relationship has become so integral to both of our worlds and our plans. If it is threatened, even fleetingly, it temporarily opens up a world of insecurity. Because we both know what pain would lie ahead if this all ended.

Character comedian Jane Postlethwaite was abruptly catapulted out of her seemingly secure life when an odd conversation on Brighton beach, followed by her partner going to stay with his brother, propelled her to check his emails. The moths of doom must have been swarming around her in a Hitchcock-ian nightmarish frenzy. 'I got really anxious because I could tell something was happening,' she says, 'So I took a diazepam and watched an episode of *Wallander*, the Swedish one with subtitles. And then something told me to get up and go and look at his laptop, something was guiding me. That lead to a pounding heart. And there it all was. He'd been meeting up with a woman he'd known for sixteen years and was planning a new relationship with her. She went off to California for six months while I had a nervous breakdown. Now he lives with her in the flat that I helped him do up.'

Jane describes feeling like 'somebody had ripped my skin off'.[1] Comedy audiobooks kept her company as she walked up and down Brighton and Hove seafront taking photos of the derelict West Pier, which seemed to mirror her 'broken down soul'.

---

1 Heartbreak can manifest in physical symptoms, including increased heart rate and body temperature, and a feeling that the skin is on fire. So Jane is not alone in this extreme sensation. For me, emotional stress triggers migraines and a compromised immune system, making me vulnerable to colds, sore throats and chest infections.

This somatic description of the pain of a breakup is similar to the imagery and language used to portray troubled courtships in the eighteenth century. According to Sally Holloway, letters, ballads and love tokens spoke of 'afflicted', 'diseased', 'plagued' and 'broken' hearts.[2] Each term was used 'in a particular way to denote the various stages of romantic breakdown. This began when the heart was cut or pierced by love, which began to pull on the heartstrings when matters took a turn for the worse. The initial injury was caused by a metaphorical weapon such as an arrow.' By the 1820s and 1830s, Valentine's Day etchings depicted suitors gleefully taking aim at one another.

Perhaps love has *always* been a battlefield.

Brilliant Irish singer-songwriter Kal Lavelle performed a powerfully affecting new song, 'Don't Know How to Live', recently on *Radio Diva*. She had separated from her partner of six years just a few months earlier and was still tending to her wounds. She explained the tension of being a creative who wants to harness the extreme hurt of the situation but also to escape it: 'The trouble with times of great change is that you're always on the brink of emotion. And as a musician, you're constantly recreating these points in your life over and over again every time you perform. But when it's so fresh, it's the last thing you want to do.'

Over sparse guitar accompaniment, she sang:

And it can hit you
At the strangest of times
I'll be doing some shopping
And end up weeping in the line
…I've got all these feelings that are so hard to describe,
Like I know that you're living but it feels as if you've died

Sometimes breakups do arrive as part of a sombre cavalcade of loss. My separation from Boozy Ex-Girlfriend was undoubtedly catalysed by the

---

2 'Broken heart syndrome' is now a recognised medical condition, with symptoms similar to those of a heart attack.

house fire, these two huge life events in turn preceded by an even more colossal one – the death of my mother. My twenties had certainly ended with quite some drama. When it came to mourning and untangling the disparate threads of grief, I felt guilty that the most intense and immediate feelings of upset were about the supposedly 'smaller' loss of my partner. She wasn't actually dead. Yet, as Kal so perfectly expresses, a breakup *is* a bereavement. Boozy Ex-Girlfriend had been a daily presence in my life for those formative years of young adulthood, more of a touchstone than my parents had been. Maybe my scale of pain isn't so out of proportion after all.[3]

After the fire, on the verge of turning thirty, I wrote a song to convey her massive significance during that era:

Today I walked past
Our burned-out flat
I know you sometimes sit outside in the car and cry
And cry
Have the neighbours moved
Nothing left of me and you
Someone painted in the cracks
In the hallway where we left our tracks
Come back
Come back
For you can be sure
You were
My life

* * *

3   I certainly wasn't alone in being a young person profoundly affected by a breakup. A 2018 Better Breakups survey by the website Status found that 48 per cent of a group of 1,000 16- to 25-year-olds said that breakups had had a negative impact on their mental health. There's something about those early breakups that really challenges the ideas we have formed about our identity. When poet Sophia Blackwell went through a breakup during her twenties, she says, 'I'd always thought I knew exactly what I wanted to be and who I wanted to be with…all that was thrown into turmoil overnight.'

The day after my tiny argument with Girlfriend about Dog, I head to Oxford Science and Ideas festival to record an episode of the podcast featuring Anna Machin. This is my chance to discover the science behind the moths of doom. Why the hell do breakups hurt so very much?

I love Oxford. Although it's a substantial walk over from the station to The Bullingdon on Cowley Road, past several of the pretty University colleges, it's exactly what I need to clear the migraine that has been threatening on the train.

'Are we all set for recording it?' I cheerily ask the sound engineer.

'I think so. I should be able to send it to you straight away if you write down your email address for me,' he says, not inspiring me with huge confidence.

Every time I take the podcast to a new venue I panic a little about the tech. What if we have an amazing discussion and it's lost forever? That's exactly what happened at the pilot event at Bradford Literary Festival. Bizarrely, we had to change venue at the last minute due to a swarm of bees.[4] So the setup at the swiftly found new place didn't quite work. A recording was sent to me. But it was unintelligible and sounded a little like a million daleks weeping. Recording has been fine ever since and I'll just have to trust that it will be again.

Jumping up onto the high stage, I rattle through some comedy and try to ignore my throbbing head. Fortunately the audience are generous. I bring Anna on and ask, 'Love has been shown to have a similar effect on the brain to when we take certain drugs like cocaine. A lot of our reward centres are lit up. So does that mean that if our lover or partner suddenly breaks up with us that we experience some kind of withdrawal?'

She responds, 'We absolutely do! One of the major neurochemicals that underpins love is beta-endorphin. It's an opiate. So it's like the body's heroin. When you're with the person you're in love with, you're existing at quite a high level of opiate in your body. So when they dump you and you have that horrible shock, then you are in fact going into opiate withdrawal, which is why it's so unbelievably psychologically and physically painful.'

'It really is,' I agree. 'I was watching a film recently called *Beautiful Boy* with Timothée Chalamet as a young guy, Nic Sheff, who is addicted

---

4 Or was it really moths of doom?!

to crystal meth. His family are trying to cope with that and help him off it. I was thinking, "I'm so glad I've never been so dependent on something." But then I thought, "Actually I have behaved in that way when I've been heartbroken, when I've needed that fix and I'm frantically calling an ex or turning up somewhere I know they're going to be." It's really very similar.'

'Oh it absolutely is. The reason we discovered that beta-endorphin is involved in heartbreak is that it was actually recognised by a psychiatrist who works with drug addicts. He realised that the way that these addicts were withdrawing and behaving was very similar to when people are in love. If you think about when you're in love, particularly at the beginning, you become completely obsessed about that person. You don't eat. You'll miss appointments. You won't concentrate at work. All the things we usually see in quite heavy drug users as well. The only thing you want is to satiate that desire for that opiate which is manifested in that person that you love. You are behaving like an obsessive addict.'

'So does it make a difference if a relationship ends abruptly after a few months while you're still in that honeymoon stage or if it breaks up when you've been together much longer?'

'It's actually harder the longer you've been together. There are lots of chemicals involved in love. You've got dopamine,[5] serotonin, oxytocin and beta-endorphin. Oxytocin and dopamine are the ones that are around at the beginning. Oxytocin is really the hormone of "lust at first sight" if you like.'

'It's a bonding chemical, isn't it?'

'Yes, but it's not good for maintaining long-term relationships because we develop a tolerance to it.'

'Like any drug, I guess!'

'...Exactly! So what we really need is a longer-term drug like beta-endorphin, which doesn't actually kick in until you've gone through those first stages of a relationship. You really only start to exist at high opiate levels when you've been together longer...so that's why if somebody dumps you after a couple of years, it can literally feel like your whole world is ending. By that stage, you're in quite an established relationship.'

---

5   Neurotransmitter that plays an important role in our reward-motivated behaviour.

'So…after about a couple of years you'd get into that beta-endorphin stage?'

'People always ask me for the timetable. And there isn't one as such. It's not like "Day forty-nine, beta-endorphin arrives…"'

'In the *Big Brother* house!'

'Yes, haha.'

'That would be a much better TV series!'

'Wouldn't it?! But people actually exist at different levels of these chemicals. Some of us are more genetically predisposed to have high levels of them. And some poor sods, about 2 per cent of the population, even carry what is known as a Gain-of-Function gene, which means that, when they split up, they feel the rejection much more powerfully. It really is the most awful, world-ending experience for them.'

'Can you test for it?'

'You can't commercially test for it. We find it when we do genetic studies. And when you speak to people it will be reflected in their relationship patterns.'

Forty minutes of fascinating conversation whizz past. I forget all about my headache and speed-walk back to the station.

On the train home, in between anxiously checking my emails for a link to the audio file, I think about our friend Zara who recently came over for tea and biscuits and shared her breakup story with me. I wonder if she'd be a prime candidate for being tested for the Gain-of-Function gene. She's certain that she has 'never been the same again' twenty years on from her first big heartbreak…

8

'Just Scream!'

Breakup Stories: 'Zara'

Zara met her first love, Jane, at a lesbian youth group when she was nineteen. They quickly became entwined in one another's lives and families. They were sure that they were 'meant to be together forever.' After living in a house belonging to Jane's parents for a couple of years, they started to make plans to buy a home together.

But then, sensing that she was also gay and a potential ally, Zara became friends with a woman called Steph at work. Steph was thirteen years her senior and unhappy in her relationship. When Jane heard about this new connection, she was excited at the prospect of going out as a foursome. But Steph split with her girlfriend before they had a chance to do so. Instead, they went out as a threesome.

Zara could immediately see Jane's attraction to Steph. 'She kept saying things like "Hasn't she got lovely eyes?" and "Doesn't she look like Amanda Burton?"[1] So we all went back to our place, having consumed a lot of wine. We were listening to the Indigo Girls. Steph was really complimenting my voice and asked me to sing. Although I wonder now if that was so she could distract me while they started getting on with it on the sofa. I got invited into it. I remember kissing Steph even though I wasn't attracted to her. I feared losing my relationship with Jane so just went along with it against my internal judgement.'

---

1 Actor Amanda Burton is probably best known for her lead role as Professor Sam Ryan on TV's *Silent Witness* between 1996 and 2004. Her signature 'reflective look into space' was lovingly satirised by Jennifer Saunders. Viewers of a certain age will also remember her as Heather from *Brookside*. Interesting note for this book: she has been through two divorces.

The new triangular relationship 'took a grip quickly'. Zara felt very much on the periphery and lost her sense of self. Over the next nine months, Steph virtually moved in. Zara and Jane did, however, make a pact that they would never see Steph separately behind each other's backs. But then one day a concerned colleague, who knew nothing of the arrangement, gently told Zara that they had seen Jane and Steph together and 'all over each other'.

Jane had broken the pact. Zara was 'beyond devastated'. She says, 'Something in my mind snapped. I knew I was going to lose her. But we were ignoring what was happening. We didn't put any words to it.' One particular evening, Zara broke the silence and asked, 'What about us? What about our plans? What about how much my parents love you?' Jane didn't know what to do, saying, 'I've fallen in love with her but I still love you too.' Zara remembers Jane seeming really vibrant and alive, while she felt dead inside. With a heavy heart, she stated, 'I can't be in a relationship where you're seeing someone else.'

Zara went to Jane's new house, the one that she had helped to choose and was supposed to move into, and collected her stuff. 'I just left a cuddly bunny in the middle of the floor. It was one of those that had a little sign saying "I love you to the moon and back". She once bought it for me I think. Then I just left and moved back in with my parents.'

However, the torture wasn't over. Zara was invited to Jane and Steph's housewarming a mere few weeks later. 'I put so much preparation into how I looked that night. I even wore some glasses with fake lenses to try and reinvent myself. I stayed for half an hour and then just hit self-destruct. I stopped eating, went out a lot and was recklessly sleeping with people. Nothing meant anything. It unlocked something in me that I haven't recovered from. My relationship with trust was impacted. I kept thinking that whoever I was with would be bound to leave and find somebody better.'

Although she 'wanted to kill' Steph, she openly forgave her and Jane…and, six years later, went along to their wedding. 'I put on a facade that I was happy. But a friend could see that I wasn't and took me off into a nearby field. She said, "Just scream!" So I did. I screamed and screamed. And I felt a bit better for it.'

Many years later, Zara had her own wedding with a woman who was her 'anchor', a stable soulmate who consistently made loving gestures that made her feel cared for and respected. Although it ended after eleven years, it did so with incredible compassion. They retained a deep friendship and Zara began a new relationship. She no longer has contact with Steph and Jane.

Meg-John Barker says, 'This story underlines how vital honesty is in all relationships. When people form open relationships, the focus is often on the relationship structure. But really we could do with focussing far less on the structure – like whether people are monogamous, non-monogamous or something in between – and much more on how people conduct their relationships of whatever kind. All types of relationship structure can work well for people, but what's vital is that they're able to communicate and to trust the others involved to be honest and ethical. It's frustrating that when non-monogamous relationships don't work, people often blame the non-monogamy because it's not the "normal" way of doing relationships in our culture. Actually huge numbers of monogamous relationships break up for the same reason – because someone is being dishonest. The issue isn't the monogamy or non-monogamy, it's the dishonesty.'

I agree with Meg-John. Triad relationships and other non-monogamous structures can work incredibly well for many people. They can sometimes even lead to a more positive and conscious outlook on breakups, something we'll revisit in the second half of this book. But the non-monogamy absolutely does have to be agreed and discussed. Even when it is, things aren't always simple.

Gay cabaret performer Luke Meredith had a pirates and brides[2] themed civil partnership ceremony with Dave eight years ago. He had experimented with open relationships before, often finding that they could end up being a 'stepping stone' towards a breakup. However, he and Dave also tried it a little while into their partnership. Luke felt that 'when you're married you need to be number one'. So when Dave met someone who became a 'more significant other', they dissolved their partnership. But they remain very good friends.

Even those of us who are sexually exclusive often have little extra-curricular crushes, harmless flirtations and fantasies. Alongside these little sparks of fleeting intrigue, the ghosts of old flames can rattle

---

2 Kate Smurthwaite turned up as a bride, just as she was going through a divorce in her real life.

around in our consciousness as we process our past stories. Girlfriend sometimes has dreams about her ex and tells me all about it the next morning. In one, she was initiating the breakup, taking a more empowered stance…whilst violently throwing up into a toilet. She was simultaneously reclaiming the narrative of the breakup and expunging it. I think it's perfectly healthy that she would still think about her ex from time to time. She spent fifteen years with this person. Whereas I can't quite work out why I am still puzzling over what happened with somebody I barely spent any time with at all…

9

The Bisexual Comedian

1 year B.G. (Before Girlfriend)

'When I meet my next boyfriend, he'll probably be the kind of guy that…'

What the fuck?!

I am so stunned by the assumed male gender of a hypothetical future partner that I don't catch the rest of this statement.

I am on a date with The Bisexual Comedian.

Or at least I think I am.

We are at a comedy party together after a few days of gentle and lovely email flirting have followed our first meeting at a gig at the BBC Television Centre. After laughing at one another's sets, we chatted among the daleks and random memorabilia. Our only subsequent face-to-face conversation time has equated to the duration of the drive in her Mini from Finsbury Park tube to the house of a comedian who lives somewhere in Crouch End. I haven't really paid attention to the name of the host or where we are exactly. We were both trying to rattle through our life stories in a few minutes. And we have both done quite a few different things.

The party is some kind of post-graduation social for participants on one of London's plethora of comedy courses, which means that many of the people here are young, white, straight dudes with whom I have nothing much to chat about. The Bisexual Comedian has begun standup in her mid-forties after establishing herself as a successful high-powered media executive and seeing her children into adulthood. Although a couple of years older than me, she is the one on an exciting new life journey. Being around her immediately connects me to my nostalgia for the early days of starting out, of being part of a fresh intake of comedians, of rallying around one another at terrible open-mic gigs.

By contrast, I am the jaded pro act caught in a wearying cycle of arrive at gig, be funny, get handed envelope of cash, go home, repeat, repeat, repeat. Lately I have been questioning what the purpose of it all is, especially now that the route to bigger, better gigs seems to be to appear on some bloodless panel show. The comedy industry is becoming exactly the type of capitalist machine that I had arrived here in order to escape from. I've been drifting away from the circuit. Many of the best friends I'd made at the start have given up and retrained in more meaningful roles as therapists or teachers.

The course tutor, my mate Kate Smurthwaite, is also here congratulating everyone on their induction into this peculiar world. I am relieved to see a familiar face from my professional peer group. So that is who we are huddled in the corner talking to when the jarring declaration of apparent heterosexuality is made. I feel confused and stupid as I take an awkward sip of wine from a plastic cup. Kate would have noticed that The Bisexual Comedian and I arrived together and that there's some kind of little dynamic or something between us.

I don't get it. She talks very freely about bisexuality onstage. It's not a secret.

I have plenty of bi women friends, many of whom are frustrated by how much more difficult it is to meet women than men. If they were talking about hypothetical partners, they'd be more likely to use a hopeful 'she' or at least a gender-neutral 'they'. I'm normally the one defending them when my old-school lesbian mates make daft sweeping biphobic statements like, 'They all end up with a man in the end.'

'That's largely due to statistics,' I'll say. 'There are a lot more straight men than queer women.' But here I am, defying the male-biased odds, a queer woman who is interested. And I'm being erased just like that. It hurts.

Yet, frustratingly, The Bisexual Comedian is one of those utterly charming people, so adept at making someone feel temporarily important, that I immediately forget how offended I am when she turns her attention back to me and snogs me in the car as she drops me off again.

'Are you sure you're into women?' I venture, 'Because it's totally cool if you're not. We can be friends.'

'Yes, yes I really am into both.'

Maybe I should bring up the 'boyfriend' comment and explain how it made me feel. But I don't want to ruin the moment. I want to savour the tiny fragment of possibility that there might be a connection blossoming. I run for the last Victoria line train and continue text flirting.

A week later, our second sort-of 'date' is an al fresco lunch in an idyllic sun-drenched pub backyard. Clearly she is having doubts.

'I worry that being in a relationship will sap me of my strength and independence. I'll be like Samson without his hair.'

Ironically, she has her long auburn hair cut off into a Mary Portas-style power bob the very next day.

And she buggers off on a work trip to Cannes, leaving me staring wistfully at the relentless carousel of positivity that is her social media.

She's one of those women with an innate sense of how to present herself and create an image. I've never had that. I just feel so uncomfortably inadequate around all that heteronormative, heteroflexible 'woman stuff'. Even though I would loosely consider myself a 'femme' lesbian, there's a certain aura of 'femininity' in the wider straight world that I feel I can't live up to. And The Bisexual Comedian is the absolute embodiment of it.

Just when she is due to return from her trip, I receive an email. The moths of doom flap around my face as I read it. Apparently I'm getting a bit 'intense' after just two dates and she isn't entirely comfortable. I guess she's used to dating men. Maybe they are really offhand and noncommittal for the first few weeks. Two lesbians, on the other hand, would've already moved in together and got a cat by the second date. As I mentioned earlier, we move quickly. But that's not familiar to her. Dating a woman who normally dates men is like dating in a foreign language. Her expectations and programming seem so entirely different.

I feel low and start to ponder why. Our brain's reward system fires not only when we receive a reward but also when we anticipate one. So if we believe that we are about to embark on a lovely new relationship and then it doesn't happen, that's a lot of thwarted dopamine[1] receptors searching for a hit. Sometimes this supposed formula, that the length of time taken to get over someone should be directly proportional to the duration of the relationship, is just not fit for purpose.

Possible futures can sometimes be more oppressive than actual memories. They don't even have to be edited to be perfect. Perhaps that explains why comedian Sarah Southern admits that she still can't bring herself to delete the messages she received from a man she had just one intense date with four years ago. She muses, 'I thought I had genuinely found "the one". It seemed he too had discovered love at first sight…but for the other girl he was seeing at the time.'

Like Sarah, I feel stunned by my sudden dismissal. What is so repugnant about me that it has become so clear after such a short amount of time? And why does it bother me so much? Who or what does The Bisexual Comedian represent?

In the 1980s, the sexologist John Money devised the phrase 'lovemap' to describe a person's internal emotional blueprint, laid down during early sexual development, defining their erotic ideals. I fear that large parts of my map may have been drawn during my first year at York University in the early 1990s. I was a fledgling, closeted lesbian, a nerdy Engineering undergrad with an unfortunate perm. Yet my desires decided to punch well above their weight and fix themselves to a woman called Kate.[2]

The first time I saw her, she was in the canteen ordering chips and a vegetarian sausage. She wore classic black Doc Martens with the addition of a tiny flower painted on the side in Tippex and had her hair pulled away from her dainty features in a quirky side ponytail. Assessing the company she was in, I figured that she was a feminist. On the spot I decided, 'I want to be a feminist, too.'

That was it. My student life was now rigidly defined around getting to know this elusive woman. I joined a collective that began to produce a women's newspaper packed with controversial articles about body image, mental health, sexual violence, periods and wanking. I took part

---

1   Even though my beta-endorphin wouldn't have kicked in yet, there was still a really tangible sense of depletion, of something missing.

2   Not Kate Smurthwaite. Or any of the other people called Kate still to come in this book. A lot of people seem to be called Kate. Except for the people I've given made-up names, obviously. I mean, I like the name Kate. But if I'd called them Kate too, we'd all be very confused.

in Reclaim the Night marches and a same-sex wedding demo, staged outside York Minster on a frosty Valentine's Day. We shivered with the thrill that we were suggesting something so radical, something that we would surely not see in our lifetimes. 'Love is not a crime,' we shouted through megaphones. Although my naive heart was breaking a little as Kate 'married' her girlfriend Sharon, I was starting to come alive. I was interested in politics, equality and what was going on in the world. When Kate stepped down as Student Union Women's Officer, I decided to stand to be her successor. My campaign, with a strong message of involving men in feminism, didn't go down well with the separatists I'd been so desperately trying to impress. But if I couldn't have Kate, it was almost as rewarding to irritate her. I was unrecognisably more driven than the feeble, directionless idiot who had been frozen by lust in the canteen months before.

Reader, I won that election.

Perhaps it was then that I fell in love with the idea of being in love with someone utterly unavailable. Because those painful, thwarted crushes are the ones that stretch you intellectually and make you bigger and better.

Kate, meanwhile, eventually got married for real…to a man. She now looks back on her time at University as her 'political lesbian'[3] phase.

Sometimes it's better not to get the girl. But if that's my life lesson, where does that leave me? Constantly pushing good people away in favour of intriguing unavailable ones? Yep, that's where…until Girlfriend, of course.

The Bisexual Comedian and I have kept in touch over the years, even though Girlfriend is a million times over a better partner for me than she could ever have been. Perhaps it's because we genuinely like each other as friendly circuit colleagues. Perhaps also because a little part of me still wants to prove that I'm not just a plaything to be dismissed so easily…and perhaps because it is way better to have allies around than enemies when you're negotiating the perils of midlife.

---

3 A political lesbian is a heterosexual feminist who chooses to present as gay in order to make an anti-patriarchal statement. The concept was proposed in the 1980s by Julie Bindel (an actual lesbian) and was still common in the early 1990s. While I understand the need to be around other women in a supportive space, young romantic me found this muddying of politics and sex really confusing.

10

Hormonal Hell

1 year 9 months A.G. (After Girlfriend)

'Jump!…Now!'

'Onto that laddery thing??'

'Yes…Go!'

'Ugh no…It's covered in moss and slime.'

'Bloody hell…You've missed it now.'

'There's another one. I can get on that. Just slow down. You're going too fast.'

'I can't control this thing if I go too slow.'

'I'm going to fall in.'

'No you won't.'

'Stop shouting!…OK…I'm on the ladder.'

'Great. Have you got the key to operate the gate?'

'Bollocks!'

This is supposed to be relaxing quality time.

Girlfriend and I have hired a Broads Cruiser from a marina near Huntingdon and plan to spend several days pootling up and down the River Great Ouse between St Ives and St Neots. Just the two of us…and Dog. The boat has the musty, cramped interior of a 1970s caravan. Washing involves sitting on the toilet, perching under a flimsy cabled showerhead whilst keeping a close eye on the rapidly flooding tray underfoot, hoping to leave enough hot water to be able to clean the plates after dinner. A tiny portable television set has an old-school booster aerial that doesn't inspire much confidence. The beds seem to be made for people even tinier than us. In a tall thin cupboard where one might hope to find a modern Hoover, there's a manual carpet sweeper that spits out as much as it removes from the threadbare beige floor. This is all a far cry from the relative luxury of our actual house.

And yet the simplicity of this existence does feel like a relief, free of the relentless tyranny of domestic admin. Here on the boat there are only basic tasks that can easily be divided up.

Whereas at home, Girlfriend often sighs, 'I'm doing *everything*!'

'Well, that's because you've added a million non-essential chores to the list without even consulting me!' I say.

Every day, people come round to give quotes for downstairs toilets, sanding floors, removing mould from the garden decking, for conservatories and new kitchens. I can't keep up with her aspiration. The house is fine. Let's just live. That's my philosophy.

And on this holiday, we can do exactly that. There are just a few things we haven't given due consideration.

First, we do not have a clue how to operate a lock. I'm in a muddle about gates, paddles, keys, buttons and ropes. What order does it all happen in? A gruff man talked us through it when we collected the boat. But I can't remember any of that now.

Second, and more importantly, we are both due on.

And once you're over forty, being due on is no laughing matter. We are not gliding around on roller skates or athletically playing volleyball as though we are in a 1990s TV ad for sanitary products. We are both entering the decade-long perimenopausal[1] stretch. Hormonal migraines, emotional upheaval and bleeding so heavy that we feel like we are menstruating for ten women rather than just one are becoming our monthly norm. We've got several more years of this before the actual menopause, which apparently will make us feel even worse. And in a lesbian relationship, the upheaval is doubled. Because there are two of you going through it.

A lesbian relationship, particularly after the age of forty, is a game of Russian roulette. Whether or not you have a good day is almost entirely governed by where you are in your cycle and where your partner is in hers.

---

1 If you're a twenty-something or thirty-something woman reading this, I'm so sorry to be the bearer of bad news. Periods often do get worse. Ugh. Let's hope that the healthcare industry starts to take women's hormonal health seriously and comes up with some proper treatments. One friend of mine has been prescribed everything from acupuncture and cranial Botox injections to antidepressants, none of it particularly effective.

It's as prudent to mark her period in your diary as your own.[2] After all, her hormonal chaos is going to have a direct impact on you…especially if you are trapped together in a very confined space, doing something stressful and unfamiliar. Even Dog has picked up on the aura of anxiety, barking and crying every time we enter one of the dreaded locks.

There is a third element compounding my sense of misplacement. It is August. I should be performing at Edinburgh Fringe – a compulsory hell for comedians. But this summer I have prioritised getting booked at other artsy festivals, Nozstock, Port Eliot and Wilderness, and am going to concentrate on writing a book proposal[3] instead. As Girlfriend settles in the cockpit behind the wheel of our underpowered, unwieldy vessel, I sit out on the front sundeck scrolling through Facebook. There are several posts from The Bisexual Comedian about selling out her show or how the shade of her lipstick matches her poster…or whatever. Somehow these declarations irritate me and fire up a silly sense of rivalry. God I hate social media. It turns out that Edinburgh Fringe month is miserable for a comedian even if you don't set foot in Scotland. What am I doing with my life? I haven't even started the book proposal.

My straight female friends of a similar age tell me that they are also experiencing some kind of crisis and often take it out on their partner. Journalist Miranda Sawyer, author of a book about midlife, says, 'It's to do with your attractiveness, your relevance and who you are. And with women there's obviously a hormonal thing as well. Perimenopause and menopause can mess with your head and can make you want to smash your relationship up into bits. One of the things that sometimes happens is you get a strong rush of sexual hormones and you might fancy someone completely inappropriate like a teacher at your kid's school. But mostly what you want to do is to break up with your old self.'

Tennis champion Chris Evert has spoken about how the menopause contributed to the ending of her eighteen-year marriage to skier Andy Mill. Women's magazines ask, 'Will your marriage survive?' While the *Daily Mail*, unsurprisingly, flips this on its head and ponders: 'Why all men should fear the menopause.' Apparently we women become

---

2 In pretty much every relationship I've had, we have what feels like a serious breakup-worthy argument almost every month, at the same time of the month. The breakup is then typically discounted when we consult our diaries and see the asterisk of doom. 'Oh well, we may as well stay together a bit longer because everything will be better next week.'

3 For *this* book. How meta is that?!

unplugged from our nurturing 'mummy' brain circuits and apply ourselves to new or long-dormant ambitions. Perhaps that is why there was a 15 per cent increase in divorce rates among the over-fifties between 2018-2019, largely initiated by women who wanted something different once they're no longer driven by needing to find the father of their children.

Yet Girlfriend and I have never even had children. Our mothering instincts attach themselves to Dog and Cat. But is that enough to hold us together through this emotional rollercoaster ride?

My friend, the brilliant cabaret artist Sarah-Louise Young, is researching menopause for a performance piece. She has spoken to many women who see this life stage as 'part of a long overdue appointment with oneself as one gets older', a sort of check-in and opportunity for reflection. The comments on her post asking: 'What do you think of when you see, hear or read the word menopause?' unsurprisingly include several colourful descriptions of the physical symptoms of bleeding, mood swings and hot flushes. Yet they seem to be far outweighed by those using more uplifting words to describe a huge psychological change that accompanies the more inconvenient physical one – 'freedom', 'relief', 'power', 'joy', 'transition', 'transformation', 'regeneration', 'celebration', 'release', 'reawakening', 'new chapter', 'new phase' and my favourite, 'Autumn queen'. This all sounds like more of a midlife rebirth than a midlife crisis. Bring it on. Some revel in 'eventually owning my own body' or being 'able to define myself as an individual, not just as an adjunct to men'.

Relationships struggle when our paths and goals diverge, when we cease to evolve at the same rate as our partner. No wonder, then, that women are outgrowing their marriages in droves and liberating themselves from a perceived stagnation and invisibility. Commenting on Sarah-Louise's thread, Christine says, 'I'm one of those statistics.' She left her husband and life in the UK to pursue a career in acting and to 'rediscover the real me. She'd disappeared. I found her again. I love her.' How can poor men possibly keep up with our renewed sense of urgency, our quest for meaning, at this critical juncture? Or, rather more pressingly for me, how can women keep up with one another? I'm a few years further along my soul-searching perimenopausal path than Girlfriend.

And, right now, that soul-searching is inspiring a fantasy where she disembarks and I abandon her on the riverbank, shouting a rapid cycle of apologies and swear words after me as I power away on a new adventure, our cruiser transformed into a slick speed boat...

The sky is getting dusky. We are pushing up to maximum velocity. We are panicking about where to moor up for the night, having already rejected one perfectly good spot. Ever the strategist, Girlfriend has printed off a detailed itinerary of dog-friendly riverside pubs, timings and distances between places of interest. But now, distracted from our original plan, we want to forge ahead to St Neots, where Angie and Liz have agreed at the last minute to join us for a picnic the next day.

'I'm looking forward to some other people turning up. You'll start being really nice again.'

Girlfriend looks wounded by my truth bomb.

A man waves and shouts as we power through his marina.

'Hey! There's a speed limit!'

'Sorry...'

There is a hellish lock near Godmanchester, where the wind sweeps across perpendicularly to your direction of travel. When we passed through it in the opposite direction, we bickered. But we have no time to faff about now. The pressure is on. I leap out more elegantly this time to open and close gates in a perfect slick system. Girlfriend and I do a high five. We have learned a new skill together, and have finally stopped fighting. Our fingers may have hovered over a metaphorical self-destruct button. But they are inching away now.

As we approach a large open park, we veer towards the mooring area. Alongside the official metal-edged concrete platform is a knobbly grassy verge.

'We can just moor up there can't we?'

Crunch crunch crunch...

'What's that?'

'Are we stuck?'

'Shit, we've run aground.'

'Look there's some people over there...hello? Can you help us...?'

Girlfriend jumps into the shallow water and starts digging the propeller out of the sandy mud with one of the mooring poles. She is in her element, saving the day by doing something physical and strong.

She looks happier than I've seen her all week. A man and a woman run over, roll their trousers up and start pushing and gently rocking the boat.

'Can you steer?'

'Errr…ohh yeah, OK.'

Soon we are moored more legitimately, thanking the helpful couple with one of our emergency bottles of Malbec and heading into town to get a takeaway curry.

As we sit at our folding picnic table, ravenously tucking in and giggling about the unusual array of pickles, I wonder how we have survived such a tetchy few days.

'It does hurt when you shout at me.'

'I know. I've been a dick. I'm sorry.'

'I'm sorry too.'

'I think I've been a bit cranky with you since our party because I didn't feel like we were equal partners in it.'

'Really?'

I thought our barbecue had been rather fun. But now I come to think of it, I suppose I was a little distracted.

11

Summer Freeze

1 year 8 months A.G. (After Girlfriend)

'I haven't forgotten about your lovely invitation and I might still make it over to your party today. I'll keep in touch. Hope you're having a great time. xx'

Two kisses. Three years on from our fleeting fling, The Bisexual Comedian still occasionally plays a subtly flirty game with me. She is single and bored. Just as I wasn't right for her, it seems nobody else is either. A string of male suitors have similarly been swiftly dispensed with. I'm slightly impressed by her resilience in holding out for the right person, where many would just settle for somebody incompatible. But I also feel odd when she toys with me like this. I still feel like I need something from her – an apology maybe. Ours was not a big breakup. Yet it still felt like one for me because of everything that it represented.

But I'm *fine* now, aren't I? I'm six months into living with Girlfriend and our Wimbledon-themed summer barbecue is in full swing. However, summer is a testing season for relationships. The so-called winter 'cuffing season', when even the most footloose cosy up with a partner between October and March, is well and truly over. The heat of July in the city makes us all feel a bit frisky.[1] Green leaves against a cloudless blue sky turn our minds to a sense of

---

1 Scientifically true! Sunlight triggers the brain to produce less melatonin, the hormone which makes us feel tired and want to stay in, and more serotonin, which makes us feel happier. For some of us, this might translate into thinking we are excited, fulfilled and optimistic all on our own and don't need that other person we've been clinging to for security all winter.

possibility.[2] Old crushes and flirtations bubble back up to the surface like steam evaporating from a baking pavement. Holiday tensions can make the summer months a peak time for breakups.

Girlfriend is rushing around with trays of canapés and topping everyone's drinks up, dressed as a giant strawberry. And I'm rather unhelpfully sitting on my arse in my tennis whites with one eye on the resumption of the men's semi-final between Nadal and Djokovic and the other on The Bisexual Comedian's message.

The key motivation for me in allowing Girlfriend to invite fifty people round is that it is a large enough number for it not to look weird to invite her. Even if she doesn't make it, it alerts her to the fact that I'm a fun person who throws fancy themed parties. The Facebook event page, which will be visible to all invited, will be full of photos of us having *fun*.

What the hell am I trying to prove? It's all a bit pathetic. But I can't help myself.

The party was supposed to revolve around the ladies final between Serena Williams and Angelique Kerber. In theory, we were supposed to chat, eat and socialise in the garden with the television on in the background for people to glance at now and then. But Wimbledon has been royally screwed up this year by Kevin Anderson and John Isner boring everyone for hours in an interminable match that tipped the second men's semi, the important one, over on to the Saturday. Several of us are crammed into the lounge watching the latest instalment of a classic rivalry play out. 'Ohhh argh nooo,' we exclaim as nasty Novak wins yet another point he had no right to.

During the sit-down between games, I wander over to the food table to get some bread and salad, remarking on people's costumes as I go. One couple have come as strawberries and cream, others as a ball, a net and a line judge, and one idiot as a streaker with a big fake plastic bottom. In the kitchen, I remove the cheese selection from the fridge. As I'm about to arrange them decoratively for everyone on a tempting platter with grapes and biscuits, I hear some excited shouts from the

---

2   Green leaves against blue sky also make me think of the cover of the 1978–90 compilation by Australian band The Go-Betweens. The album spans their career from their beginnings in Brisbane to their 1989 breakup, a band split that also prompted multi-instrumentalist Amanda Brown to end her romantic partnership with one of the two main songwriters, Grant McLennan. McLennan and co-founder Robert Forster reformed the band in 2000 before McLennan sadly died in 2006.

lounge. So I head back in to join my friends, taking the cheeses with me to unwrap in front of the television.

Girlfriend swoops in and grabs the packet of cheeses.

'Aren't you going to put them out for everyone?'

'I was just about to.'

She tuts and leaves the room to arrange the cheeses.

'Can I just take a bit of the Saint Agur to spread on my bread?'

She fires me her 'yet again, I'm doing *everything*' look. But she brings it on herself. Surely the party didn't need to be anywhere near this elaborate, with fancy caterers, multiple menu options and Wimbledon-themed balloons, plates and cutlery. My friends would be happy with booze and crisps. Her logic is that nobody should enjoy their own party. The satisfaction comes from the success of everyone else having enjoyed it.

After the match finishes, we play some soft tennis on the front drive where Girlfriend has set up a dummy court (OK, yes, she probably *is* doing everything). Every time I hit a good shot, I imagine The Bisexual Comedian walking up the road seeing me having lots of *fun* and thinking how *fun* I am and what a great *fun* best friend I would make. I wonder how present I have really been with all of our actual friends…the ones who have turned up.

As Girlfriend and I tidy up clanking empty bottles and half-eaten veggie burgers in the early hours, she asks, 'Do you *like* parties?'

An image springs to mind and surprises me…a sad little torn invitation with faded green crimped corners. I don't like parties and I've just remembered why. A party is a pretty clear way for your entire peer group to alert you to the fact that they don't like you.

'When I was in the sixth form, I tried to throw an eighteenth-birthday do but everyone tore up the invitations in my face.'

I had buried this. But it's true. They all boycotted it, even many people I had regarded as friends. A few brave mates crossed the picket line and fed me booze to help me not notice the barren emptiness of the dancefloor. It was some evil concoction called a Red Witch which made me puke bright scarlet threads of saliva onto my white top on the minibus home.

This is a curveball for Girlfriend too. She looks stunned.

'Bastards! I'm sorry that happened to you, baby.'

Restless and hot in bed, I feel a familiar scratchy sensation at the back of my throat. The stress of socialising has caught up with my body. I'm about to be ill.

My mind wanders back to the exclusion I felt at school.[3]

In my half-dreamed memory, my cheery former art teacher Mr Turner Blu-Tacks a series of insipid teenage self portraits to the classroom wall. His beard twitches with excitement as mine comes to the top of the pile.

'Ooh…and what do we all think of this one?'

The homework assignment had been to explore chiaroscuro. My peers have all used contrast to strangely soften themselves, smooth their jagged edges.

Yet I have produced a piece of pure Gothic horror. A gnarled expression of fear and self-loathing contorts my candlelit face, which in turn melts away into a background of an imagined series of constrictive, progressively smaller archways.

The class is stunned. I have marked myself out as different yet again. It's something I've tried to fix ever since – the fact that all my friends broke up with me.

---

3   A 2003 UCLA study by Matthew D. Lieberman and Naomi Eisenberger found that social rejection triggers the same alert as a primal threat. If the tribe excludes us, our survival is threatened. For me, this rejection meant a social, if not actual, death…for the remainder of the academic year at least. But perhaps it is no wonder that breakups and rejections might be triggering for me with this hurtful experience lurking in my psyche.

12

The Friendship Breakup

Breakup Stories: Eva Bindeman

'At least my romantic breakups can't possibly be as bad as this.'

A decade ago, Bristol comic Eva Bindeman met her friend Lizzie at university. They didn't get along at first as they were seemingly so different: 'I was from a farm in Northumberland and she was from money in Essex. She was training to be a doctor whereas I studied theology and am now a nanny and aspiring comedian.'

But these differences ultimately became something to celebrate, as they grew into part of a wider friendship group and, eventually, best mates. However, they fell out on Lizzie's wedding day, where Eva was due to be maid of honour.

'I was on my way to Essex and I got a call saying my grandmother was in hospital. My gran and I were extremely close and I was the only person who could get to her that day. My mum lives in Spain, my aunt in Ireland, my sister in LA and my brother was in Portugal at the time. I drove to Lizzie's house to explain and apologise that I might not make the wedding after all. She was very cold, disappointed and hurt.'

Eva was by her gran's side as she agreed to put her in palliative care. The rest of her family arrived the next day and they all stayed together while her gran died. By that time, Eva had of course missed the wedding. Lizzie would not talk to her.

Eva wished her well and removed her former friend from social media. She describes feeling 'hurt, alone and lost'. She didn't even feel she could lean on the rest of the friendship group in case it made them uncomfortable and like they had to choose a side. She grew apart from them too.

She now wonders if friendship 'is seen as a more disposable kind of love'. We don't have the same kind of recognised cultural script for mourning the loss of a friendship as we do for grieving a romantic relationship. There aren't any heart-rending ballads about pining for your former best friend. And, worst of all, we lose the exact person we would want to turn to in a crisis. Heartbreakingly, they are the source of the pain.

Author and journalist Kate Leaver researched friendship breakups for a chapter of her lovely book *The Friendship Cure*. Many of the people who came forward with stories had never opened up about these endings before because they 'simply didn't know how to grieve them'. She found that the most common things people said were that it felt 'like a death' and 'even more personal than a romantic breakup'.

Kate explains, 'With romantic relationships, most of us are just looking for one partner so there's just one spot to be filled. So if you get rejected because you're not "the one", then that's kind of OK. However, we can have infinite numbers of friends. So if someone goes to the trouble of getting to know you and then says, "You know what, I could have as many friends as I like, but I do not want *you* in my life", that's way more offensive. It feels so very crushing when it happens to you.'

Kate advises that we should give ourselves permission to feel hurt and upset when a friendship ends. Although there isn't the same socially sanctioned healing time awarded to us, we can give it to ourselves: 'Pour an extra little bit of love and attention into your remaining friendships, eat ice cream, go for long walks, have a big angry cry, bring out all your favourite coping mechanisms and then find a way to move on.'

Performer and academic Naomi Paxton agrees that friendship breakups are the ones that really weigh on her. Her romantic life has been incredibly free of drama. 'There was no storming off, poison pen letter or smashed vase. I don't think I've ever had anything spectacular. Everything was so vanilla back then, there was nothing to regret,' she says, giggling one night over dinner. But recalling a story about the loss of a good friend, her habitually jolly veneer ebbs away a little and she becomes more reflective and remorseful than I've ever seen her.[1]

In her late twenties, Naomi moved in with a gay male friend who she met while working on the live show *Chitty Chitty Bang Bang*. They were 'super-close' and 'in each other's pockets'. He had come out as gay when he was sixteen. So he was able to be a huge support in her coming-out process. This bonded them tightly. But then Naomi became overly protective and jealous when he got a new boyfriend: 'I worried for him when I heard them arguing. But I was too close to it. I'd become too reliant on him for my emotional wellbeing.' One night it all came to a head, doors were slammed and he moved out.

However, a few years later when she met her wife Kathryn, something happened that offered a fresh perspective on the breakup. A close male friend of Kathryn's became jealous of the new relationship. Naomi saw the behaviour and realised, 'This is what I was doing with my friend. I behaved badly but it was from a place of love but also a place of hurt and a desire for nothing to change. That was part of my story and not generous to him. It's sad isn't it that you have to learn by making mistakes?'

Friendships and romantic relationships can sometimes jostle for position in uncomfortable ways. In my comedy show *Is Monogamy Dead?* I ponder whether friendship is perhaps the only pure, rational form of love, unclouded by the involuntary chemical reactions of lust. We *choose* to spend time with our friends. Whereas, we choose to *fuck* our partners. And when we get those things muddled, we fuck up.

I sometimes wonder if the disappointment I feel about my stuttering fling with The Bisexual Comedian is really that it might have corrupted a genuine chance to make a great new friend. What I desired even more than a sexual connection was for us to drive into the sunset as feminist gal pals like Thelma and Louise.[2] She represented an even bigger psychological script for me. She was my chance to sellotape those torn green-fringed party invitations back together and become popular again. Popular, like her.

---

1 What a pest I am, constantly prodding my friends for sad stories and bringing their mood down. If I'm not careful, they'll all be breaking up with me. On this occasion, my guilt is assuaged by the fact that we have made Naomi and Kathryn a slap-up feast on the barbecue. And after dinner, Dog brings us all back to hilarity as she has an unfortunately public upset-tummy incident.
2 OK, not *quite* like Thelma and Louise.

But how do you even ask someone to be friends? Just as there is no script for the demise of a platonic love, there is no opening line either.

I had just assumed that we would follow the queer women's rulebook and become besties when any potential romance fizzled out. It had always been something of an unspoken code in my lesbian circles in the 1990s. An alliance forged in the face of prejudice was important. Any type of connection with a fellow 'sister' was precious. In fact, many of us deliberately slept together as a fast track to enduring platonic love.

Yet, as a woman who has dated men for most of her life, she follows a different protocol.

It's a shame. During my first year with Girlfriend, even though I'd finally found the romantic partner I'd been searching for, I desperately needed someone else to turn to sometimes. I craved someone who understood my professional world...

13

Only Child Syndrome

9 months A.G. (After Girlfriend)

'Come home, baby. This is bullshit. You're better than this.'

These are not the words that any comedian wants to hear their visiting partner utter when they are a few days into an Edinburgh Fringe run.

We are sitting on the grass drinking overpriced takeaway teas at the top of Calton Hill looking across the city with the odd Athenian-style pillared National Monument of Scotland to our right. Edinburgh sun has an altogether chillier feel than London sun. But at least it's not raining.

I feel an overwhelming ache of loneliness. I know that I have to make the best of this month of hell away from home, even though I'm rundown, exhausted and have made a terrible choice of venue. I had hoped that broken microphones, primitive lighting systems and falling-down backdrops were behind me. I have played some nice venues at the Fringe – Assembly Hall, Underbelly, The Voodoo Rooms, even music-oriented Sneaky Pete's on Cowgate had a really fun vibe. But this year, my sensitive, lovingly crafted storytelling show is completely at odds with the sticky pub attic I find myself in. It feels something of a comedown from my tours of well-equipped festivals and pristine arts centres.

I long for an ally, one who wants to help me figure out how to make the untenable tenable. Yet Girlfriend thinks that the best way to support me is to tell me to quit. It's not. Even if my solo show is a near write-off, there will be guest slots, networking and a million other reasons to stay on in the horrid flat miles out of town that I've already paid thousands of pounds to live in for three weeks.

My sadness is compounded when we pop into Naomi Paxton's show. In character as monstrously funny magician's assistant Ada Campe, she weaves a mystical tale of a psychic duck with dancing, audience participation, tricks and silliness. Her wife Kathryn, also an actor, is behind the tech desk operating the sound and lights with the precision of someone that is utterly invested in the show. Partners who are also performers understand the way that Edinburgh works. It's all hands on deck. Everyone mucks in. The acts who have the most success rope in parents, siblings, children and friends to hand out flyers, put up posters and help with the horrific stress of it all. But I have nobody. That might have been alright, if I'd known. But I thought I had somebody. I thought I had Girlfriend.

The extreme world of Edinburgh Fringe is forcing me to believe in an extreme version of monogamy where my partner suddenly has to become my manager, publicist and technician on top of being my lover. Even I don't think she should be all those things. But I'm so exhausted and wretched from having to do all those things myself for so many years. It's just too much.

I have always longed for a creative 'wife', an artistic soulmate who wants to take on the comedy world together. I always feel super-jealous when I read about Phoebe Waller-Bridge and her 'love-affair friendship'[1] with Vicky Jones, who directed the first stage version of *Fleabag* at Edinburgh Fringe in 2013. I had a brief taste of a rewarding professional partnership when I began my first ever podcast *Odd Ones Out* in 2012 with my friend Rachel. It was a satirical, queer take on current affairs full of malapropisms, weirdly named episodes like 'Pride Comes Before a Falling Platypus'[2] and misnamed political figures, like North Korean leader Mel il-Kim and Labour Party brothers Ed and David Millipede, who still couldn't get a foot in the door at Ten Downing Street despite having hundreds of legs. It was a creative playground where we had the freedom to say what we liked, often collapsing into heaps of giggles,

---

1   'Love-affair friendship' is a term I discuss at length in my first book *Is Monogamy Dead?* It describes the sort of close, platonic female bonds that are, for many women, stronger, longer lasting and more important than those with their husbands and sexual partners. Yet these friendships often support romantic relationships by taking some of the burden of expectation away. A large proportion of needs are met by the friend. So they are more likely to assist a partnership by relieving pressure rather than threaten it and break it up. This is loosely a sort of polyamorous setup, even where the sexual partnerships are exclusive.

2   That week, an Australian man had been jailed for dropping a statue of a platypus on his gay flatmate.

rendering some episodes completely useless. Yet Rachel became very poorly soon after our first and only live show, something we discussed in the episode 'Two Weddings and a Transplant'. There was no way we would be able to put in the hard-graft touring and self-promoting that I would be able to on my own. So we remained friends and I continued on my lonely solo professional journey.

I often wonder if my feelings of isolation and difficulties in maintaining all types of relationships, platonic, professional or romantic, are rooted in my growing up as an only child. The myth of 'only child syndrome' originated in the early 1900s when a flawed study attributed a long list of negative, antisocial traits to us sibling-free folks. Although these findings were subsequently disproved by more recent research, the myth still persists. Perhaps both sets of research are sort of right. Only children are becoming more and more common. In the UK, 40 per cent of married couples have just one child. And that figure is higher for single-parent families. Modern only children will be absolutely fine because they no longer seem 'strange' or out of the ordinary.

Yet back in the 1970s, when I was an only child, I was one of only about 11 per cent. It was a bit weird to not have siblings. It was one more way in which I was a minority. It did make me a target for bullying, especially when compounded by the other looming dark cloud of difference, that of being gay. And guess what? Being bullied does make you close off from people just a tad. So then when someone kind finally does come along and bursts through these defences with a genuine desire for connection, an overload of expectation is put on that person. 'Here they are…my rescuer, at last!' And that intensity often leads to relationship burnout and a breakup.

Furthermore, when researchers at Ohio State University studied 57,000 adults between the years 1972 and 2012, they found that only children were more likely to divorce. Apparently, each sibling reduces the likelihood of a separation by 2 per cent. Co-author of the paper, Lisa Marie Bobby, attributes this to 'greater experience of dealing with others.'

'So when we get married, I'll be 4 per cent less likely to get divorced than you because I've got two brothers?' asks Girlfriend quizzically.

'Haha, yes, I see your point. It doesn't make sense that it isn't an equal probability…because if I get divorced then you do too. But maybe it means that I'll be more likely to be the one initiating it.'

She doesn't seem too impressed with this suggestion. But right now, I feel so alone that any hypothetical wedding plans are well and truly cancelled in my mind. In the dingy, cramped bedroom, we restlessly try to sleep at the outer opposite edges of the lumpy bed, a powerful magnetic force pushing us apart. Stealthily googling 'when partner doesn't support your dreams', I alight upon a *Harvard Business Review* article with the bold heading: 'If You Can't Find a Spouse Who Supports Your Career, Stay Single'. Is this the flick of the switch, the moment of clarity that signals that, for all Girlfriend's wonderful qualities, she is still not 'the one' for me? Are we about to break up? The moths of doom are hovering, poised for full flight.

Yet my loneliness isn't nearly so simple or binary. Former Surgeon General of the United States and now author, Dr Vivek Murthy, talks about loneliness having three dimensions: intimate, social and collective. It's all too easy to blame our lack of social connection (friendships) or collective connection (people who share similar goals) on our partner, even when our intimate connection with them is actually very strong and deeply fulfilling. My exhausting pattern of serial monogamy, and lots of breakups, has been driven by a mistaken belief that there might be one single person out there who can heal the fractures in *all* of my dimensions of connection. There isn't. Even though the seemingly alluring, possibility-filled world of singledom might open up avenues for new friendships, career opportunities or at least a transient August lover who knows how to work a sound desk, would these tiny fairy steps forwards be worth the huge stride backwards it would be to lose an honest, kind partner whom, ultimately, I do…y'know…*love*?

The next morning, a lovely four-star review of my show appears online and brightens the mood…as does a standing-room-only appearance at Edinburgh Book Fringe at Lighthouse Books on West Nicolson Street. Billed as 'an activist, intersectional, feminist, lgbtq+ community space', of course it's the type of place that my core audience are going to happily come to. As they guffaw along to the story of my awkwardly chaste visit to the lesbian sauna, my collective loneliness washes away. This is my tribe.

It's not that straight people don't enjoy my material. They really do. Once they make it through the door. In her solo show *Out Of Sync*, Maureen Younger acknowledges comedy's unconscious bias: 'Most comics in Britain talk about themselves. The norm in standup has historically been a white straight man. So if he comes onstage and talks about stuff, he'll be judged solely on whether or not he is funny. It is expected that the content of what he has to say is of interest to everyone. It's not the same if you're black, gay or a woman. If I go on and talk about myself, it's no longer the norm…because I'm banging on about being a woman. And it's only of interest to other women, a few gay men and possibly the odd vegan.'

The intensely competitive nature of Edinburgh amplifies this problem. Outside of the select few acts being talked up by the critics, anyone telling a non-normative story is going to get smaller audiences and make less money on ticket sales. Coupled with that, the criminally exponential increase in short-term August rents excludes pretty much anyone without a posh family to bankroll them. Inventive no-budget guerrilla marketing and imaginative publicity stunts have been replaced by officious, combative street teams. The whole city has been commercialised to within an inch of its life, a price tag attached to every lamp post, phone box or shop window. Many comics feel that, far from being the 'open access' festival that it purports to be, the Fringe has come to perpetuate a heteronormative system of privilege and power. As Maureen asks, 'Is it time to fit in or just revel in your own eccentricity?'

Over Italian food, I regale Girlfriend with previous tales of Fringe woe, of flooded venues, ruined posters and absent 'producers'. And I realise that, once I've done what I can to salvage this August, I'm going to extricate myself from the mother of all abusive relationships, one that I have kept on returning to year after year. I'm going to break up with Edinburgh Fringe.

I need to break up with something, to shed some pain. And this is a far healthier choice than leaving Girlfriend would be.

Does this count as an abusive relationship? If so, we can tick off the final item on Kathy's list. We have a full house of breakups. Hooray!

I feel like it really does count. Edinburgh is a bad lover who stole all my money and made me feel like shit about myself for years. It's no accident that the worst flashpoints in my human relationships, particularly with Secretive Ex-Girlfriend, happened during August.

This sorry, wasted month feels just as devastating as any relationship breakup. I had prepared my show so thoughtfully.

14

Unwanted Snapshots

7 months A.G. (After Girlfriend)

What Does Heartbreak *Look* Like?

'I'm going to step out of the room for a minute. I want you to create an image that conveys heartbreak using the objects available in this room. Let me know when you're ready for me to come back in.'

I'm having a mentoring session at the home of brilliant performance artist Stacy Makishi, investigating ways of adding extra elements to my solo show about breakups. As a standup and writer, I'm so focused on text that I often forget about what a performance looks like. What visual cues might describe something more economically than words?

The first time I witnessed a breakup, I was seventeen. We were at an eighteenth birthday party, one that everyone had decided to go to.

A sweet blonde boy called Calvin openly wept on the sticky steps leading up to the dancefloor at a club in Southport, having just been abruptly dumped. The happy-clappy disco music seemed at odds with his emotional display. Tears rolled onto his crisp, clean jeans. He couldn't wipe them away quickly enough. They just kept on coming. One of the girls broke away from the huddle around his new ex to comfort him when it became clear that the boys weren't going to. I wondered if I would ever be allowed to feel things, openly like that, in public. I was well aware of my status as a total nobody back then, an invisible outsider observing from the sidelines.

Although I can't recreate a late-1980s North-West nightclub in Stacy's living room, there's a sense of how heartbreak prompts us to look back, to reassess and rewrite our personal histories. How can I reflect that?

Thinking on my feet like this is familiar. Ad-libbing and heckler put-downs are all part of my job. But as I scan the boxes of knick-knacks, vases, jars, flowers, toys, cushions, pens and paper, my mind is temporarily blank. Then I spot something that seems unusually old-fashioned – an envelope stuffed full of photographs of smiling, laughing groups of friends at parties and events. I lie on the floor carefully scattering the images over myself, concealing my entire body and face. I am submerged, suffocated by an avalanche of memories. Technically these are Stacy's memories. But the principle is the same.

Clinical psychologist Janice Hiller says that the mistake many of us make after a breakup is to dwell on only the good memories of the relationship, the happy, smiling snapshots. This is all too easy in the era of social media, with unwanted memories and anniversary prompts popping up all the time. If we feel that we have lost the 'perfect' partner or friend, then the pain can be immobilising. Whereas if we recall the spiky conflicts, misunderstandings and frustrations, then it becomes easier to move forwards and believe that there might well be someone and something better ahead. This is sometimes known as a 'negative reappraisal' strategy[1] and has been used to help alcoholics in treatment. When they think about the negative consequences of drinking, they are more likely to give up.

Stacy's next exercise is for me to go into the kitchen and create an 'action' that represents the feeling of my show. I select a giant French coffee cup, fill it to the brim with water and carry it gingerly towards where she is sitting, silently imploring her to take it from me without spilling a drop. The round surface of fluid wobbles ominously as I lower it with care into her hands.

'Oh Rosie, thank you…that's powerful.'

---

1 I'm pretty sure this is what Becky was doing when she came round for dinner and said that she had been 'unhappy for the entire three years' that she was with Lena. It seems a more comforting narrative when you have broken up with someone.

Stacy immediately understands the metaphor. Love is such a fragile, messy thing. Sometimes we are too trusting. Sometimes we hand over too much, too quickly for the other person to receive and cope with. We place an overwhelming burden of responsibility on the keeper of our inner desires.

It's Stacy's turn to create an action. She slowly unwinds a roll of toilet paper around us, binding us together, both sitting perfectly still on the floor like a couple of codependent mummies. Immobilised again.

'How was your session?' asks Girlfriend, as she picks me up in the car later.

'It was so fun.'

'I can't wait to see the new version of the show. I love watching you perform.'

'Aww. You haven't always loved it though, have you? It was a bit stressful for you in the beginning, wasn't it?'

'You mean when you were publicly discussing our sex life?'

'Haha, yeah, that.'

15

Sex and Death

1 month A.G. (After Girlfriend)

'I might try some new material tonight about…um…y'know…being in a new relationship…'

'Haha, is it going to be about me? Remember I'm quite a private person. But I trust you. I'm sure you'll make it funny.'

The beginnings of a sexual connection with a new lover are a richly comedic time, particularly when you are both women, from the anxiety around missing the memo about a new pubic hairstyle[1] coming into fashion to the ridiculous reactions of overly curious male friends. Although when Girlfriend told one colleague about the marathon length of one of our early seduction sessions, his first response was not the standard enquiry into the mechanics of lesbian sex but… 'Did you order a pizza?' What he was forgetting was that women can multitask. Girlfriend did manage to pan-fry some sea bass on the side amidst all the action.

Lena's comedy night is held in a dingy Soho basement bar called She. Rising London rents, the growth of apps and online culture, alongside a queer female tendency to couple up then disappear into domestic bliss for a few years until a breakup drives them out into the wild again, have forced lesbian bars, quite literally, underground. We are a difficult, inconsistent audience to cater for. I long for the 1990s when you could have a drink with gay people and actually look out of a window. She bar's

---

1   In the 1990s, when I got together with Boozy Ex-Girlfriend, a fairly full 'muffro' was perfectly acceptable. However, when I emerged from that relationship, this was no longer the case. My first post-breakup shag was with a glamorous younger woman. I was horrified to find that the fashion was now for a neat, tiny 'landing strip' of hair. I had to run to the bathroom for some emergency pruning. Thank goodness she removed her pants first, the brazen hussy.

latest refurb has only added to the subterranean bunker feel, with a tin roof lining the sweaty arched caves. Still, the place is absolutely packed and has reasonably good acoustics for amplifying laughter. I feel a little rush of adrenalin. Testing out new material can always be a rollercoaster, even without the added element of a new partner watching on. I don't want to fuck up in front of Girlfriend.

'Rosie! Rosie! Rosie!...' chants an enthusiastic regular at London lesbian standup nights. A Frenchwoman named Sylvie, she must know all of our sets off by heart now. Perhaps it's been a good way to learn English.

Becky leaps up from her perch behind the sound desk, arms outstretched for a hug with her headphones falling out of her ears, delighted to see me and already quite pissed. We have only met a few times so far. Yet her company feels easy.

'Hey Wilbybeast! Where's the short, Welsh ginge?'

'Oh she's just gone to the bar…Do you want anything?'

'No thanks, I'm fine,' she beams, reaching for two beers, one for each hand.

'Are you doing the sound?'

'Yeah. I really want to support the night. The last few have all been so good. I think we can really grow it and take it to a bigger venue.'

Lena squeezes her way through the bustling crowd to welcome me and pass me a drinks voucher.

'It will be fun tonight, I think! I start in a few minutes.'

'I'll be ready. Well done on getting such a lot of people out on a Sunday. This is a great atmosphere!'

'Did you hear you were on our last podcast?'

'Oh…the last one? Are you stopping doing it?'

'Oh no, this is a painful English lesson… I mean, it was our *latest* one.'

'Haha oh yay, that's good news. I'll listen out for it.'

Girlfriend makes her way to the back to hide away at the end of the bar while I hover in an alcove just behind the makeshift stage area. She looks anxious on my behalf. I reach over with the voucher in case she needs to get herself a stiff drink to handle the stress.

Lena's opening compèring routine seems to be based largely around her apparently disastrous love life. Becky jovially shrugs as if to say, 'I'm not getting a very good review here!'

'…And now please welcome a good friend of mine who is very funny…It's Rosie Wilby…'

'Thank you…thank you so much…oh so I'm a bit tired actually… because…I've been having sex!'

The audience cheer…although a few heads have immediately turned to stare at Girlfriend. She is pressing herself backwards into the wall as if becoming part of the strange arched bunker.

How do they all even know that she is the lover I'm going to be talking about? I thought our pre-show kisses were fairly discreet. Obviously not!

'I've realised that the difference between sex in your forties and sex in your thirties is that you need an afternoon nap first…'

The lesbians all laugh generously as I talk them through my sex warm-up exercises and lunges and tell a silly, unnecessarily elaborate story about how a trip to the local corner shop takes on a different energy altogether when one still has giveaway 'messy bed hair'. Although it ultimately turns out that the neighbours all think I'm a woman on the verge of a breakdown rather than a 'sex bomb reactivated'.

Nevertheless, out of the corner of my eye I see Becky give Girlfriend a silent fist bump for providing the inspiration for this erotically charged new set.

'It turns out I'm quite posh during sex…My libido went missing in action for two years, came back talking like a Jane Austen character… 'Where have you been libido?'…'I don't know but let's see if we can't take a turn about the grounds and get lost in the maze…'

I'm in my element, running about the tiny stage, acting out all of these daft scenarios. Yet as I take my final bow, there's a hum of dissonance ringing in my ears. Although this material is fun, it isn't as meaningful to me as the subtler, sadder, sensitive shows full of psychology, surveys and stats that I've been touring about breakups and infidelity. There's an unresolved question nagging away at me. Is the stuff I really want to do actually still comedy? And if it isn't, will my soul get eaten away by the need to be a performing monkey, too desperate for laughs to follow her heart? I yearn to write a book. Then I can demonstrate that I can do both serious and funny. My friend has just become an agent. She is my chance. But it feels scary. What if I do find a way to unleash all the things that I really want to say about how messed up human relationships are…and nobody cares, nobody changes their behaviour, the world just keeps on turning and everything stays the same. What if we all just keep ghosting each other?

Becky breaks my temporarily dark post-gig thoughts with a congratulatory hug.

'Hey you were brilliant!'

'Aw, thanks mate. It was fun.'

Girlfriend shakes her head, smiling.

'I have no words.'

'Are you alright…?'

'Yes, baby, you were very funny. I was just a bit spooked when everyone turned around to look at me.'

'Haha, yes, I hadn't expected that.'

'At least I came out of it quite well.'

Becky laughs. 'You came out of it way better than I did. You two are so cute together. Awww…'

We have had such a great evening. I can't wait to get home with Girlfriend, hold her and kiss her. Yet as we run for the train at Charing Cross, the darkness hovers over me again. I have to top up my Oyster card and it adds on critical seconds before we reach the platform. The beeping sound of the doors closing alerts us to the fact that we are too late as we breathlessly slow-motion run towards the already departing train. I feel as if I have failed a test. Everything is supposed to be a success tonight. Missing the train isn't part of the equation. It shouldn't matter. There's another in fifteen minutes. But for no reason I just start swearing. A rage comes out. All the times I have felt ignored, coerced, bullied, invisible. It's all there, all the ugliness.

'Fucking idiots, why did they drive the train off early?'

Girlfriend looks shocked and walks to the other end of the platform.

'I can't be with you if you're like this.'

Shit. Is this over already? Does she mean she can't be with me…*at all?*

I give her a few minutes then tiptoe towards her. The moths of doom are circling.

'I'm sorry. I don't know where that came from.'

'If that's you, then I'm not sure I can do this.'

'It's not me. It's just this weird job. I find it stressful sometimes. I don't know why. Please can we still go home together and spend some time together and just chill.'

'Give me a minute.'

I back off and wait for the train in silence.

I hope so fervently, so passionately that this first stupid argument isn't fatal.

The train arrives. I plead under my breath that she will board it, too. 'C'mon baby…'

She gets on. Thank fuck for that.

As we move off, we gently touch hands, reconnecting but not speaking, gazing out at the city lights.

I think of a similarly silent journey on a coach across Australia with Secretive Ex-Girlfriend. We had been to see my cousin Christopher in Canberra. After a month with her friends, one night with my own family seemed like a small ask. A few years older, Chris had been my idol while I was growing up. He seemed so handsome, cool and fun, the older brother I had always wanted. This seemed like my only chance to see him again, and meet his wife and children, in all the years since he had emigrated.

Yet Secretive Ex-Girlfriend had seemed grouchy and resentful. To try and cheer her up, I'd given her half of the money I'd received at my gigs, so we could enjoy spending it together on food and drink. Disappointingly, she lost all 500 dollars. Someone must have grabbed the wad of cash while she slept.

Normally I would've kept my eyes on the money. Instead I was distracted. Chris had lifted up his T-shirt to show me the scars left by his successful operation and treatment for bowel cancer. And he had said something strange.

'I don't blame your mum for stopping her treatment.'

I hadn't ever thought that Mum had been given much of a choice. Chemotherapy and surgery certainly wouldn't have been a tantalising option. But I wasn't even aware there had been a discussion.

As the illuminated Southwark tower blocks creep past and the late-night train fog of beer and chips transports me back from the dusty, orange Aussie soil and air-conditioned bus, I wonder…was this the biggest breakup of all, the big abandonment that I had been searching for answers about? Understandable as it was, given the odds of success and the nature of the treatment, Mum had chosen to die.

Perhaps if a breakup is similar to a death, then a death is also similar to a breakup. In my head, an early episode of the podcast begins to play back. In it, Matthew Baylis, who turned to comedy to 'get out of the house' in later life after selling his business, speaks about losing his wife to cancer a decade ago.

They got together in their final year at university, had six children together and were married for twenty years, a partnership he describes as 'wonderful, happy and balanced'. When she died, he suddenly had 'six other heads to try and sort out as well as my own'. Yet he 'dusted himself down' and eventually married again seven years ago. He is ready to travel 'into the sunset' with his new love, now that all the children are grown up.

Although he had his first big relationship end in the most tragic way, he still says, 'I'm not absolutely certain you should have one relationship all the way through. If you have kids, it's a different person to who you met before you have kids to who it is you have kids with and, by the end of that process, a lot of people split up when the kids get a bit older. People change. Circumstances change as well. I think that's the way of it. You have one relationship for a period of time then another relationship for another period of time. I think I'm just going to have the two and that'll be cool.'

I find his philosophical acceptance of events incredibly touching. It feels so much more evolved than my terrible difficulty in dealing with things beyond my control.

'What are you thinking?' ventures Girlfriend.

'Well, first of all I'm hoping that you're alright because I desperately don't want to lose someone who sees me, someone I have connected with and fallen in love with so deeply…'

'Oh well, I'm OK, thanks…we're going to be alright.'

'Phew…and then I was wondering how I should have felt about my mum stopping cancer treatment.'

'Oh wow OK…I thought your dad said she had treatment?'

'She did have an operation and some treatment the first time round. But I think maybe when it came back, she opted out…I feel quite fuzzy on it as it wasn't communicated to me all that clearly. I was still just a kid really. How about you when your dad died?'

'Oh god, I was in complete denial that he was going to die. I thought he'd get better. I was living away from home, full of my own self-importance.'

'Didn't you come out to your mum around that time?'

'Yes. I told her I was gay in the gap between him dying and the funeral.'

'Oh crap, probably not the best timing.'

'No, she didn't want to talk about it.'

'And didn't you leave your girlfriend soon after that?'

'Yes, she was my first girlfriend. We'd been together two or three years after I finished uni. We were living together in London, starting out on our careers. She was lovely and we had a nice friendship. But something had changed after my dad died. She went away to Barcelona when I was grieving.'

'Yeah I was living with my first proper girlfriend when Mum died and it totally changed things for us too. I mean, there were other things like her drinking and stuff. But we were still getting on OK until then. It just changes us, doesn't it?'

'Losing someone?'

'Yeah.'

'I know I stayed in my next relationship way too long because I couldn't cope with another ending.'

'I can understand that. I think I've struggled with endings ever since. Because that one was so beyond my control.'

'Oh shit, baby…'

'What? What have I said..? Have I upset you?'

'No…this is our stop…we've got to get off.'

'Oh yes…crap…OK.'

As we alight together and stroll back to her flat, I realise that our common imperfections and the parts of our histories that painfully overlap are what make us so right for one another.

For all the sexual chemistry, playfulness, honesty, compassion and joy we share, this mutual understanding of a similar ghost of grief might be the thing that means that we will never, ever break up.

Part Two
Bonus Breakup Content

Breakup Playlist

As chosen by my podcast guests, friends and ex-girlfriends

What Does Heartbreak *Sound* Like?

'Go Your Own Way' by Fleetwood Mac (chosen by me): How else would you start a breakup playlist? This classic 1976 pop song, penned by Lindsey Buckingham as a fairly clear message to fellow band member and ex Stevie Nicks that he felt better off without her, was my walk-on music for my solo show, *The Conscious Uncoupling*.

'Two out of Three Ain't Bad' by Meatloaf (chosen by Sofie Hagen, comedian and podcaster): 'When I was younger I allowed myself to be in relationships I didn't really want to be in. At sixteen, I was with this guy I just didn't know how to break up with. He sent me a Britney Spears song and said, "This is how I feel about you." I thought, "That's a good idea." So I sent him Meatloaf to express how I felt about him.'

'Tomorrow' by James (chosen by Suzy Bennett, comedian): 'To me, the chorus means to remind yourself to not hold onto something or someone too tightly if it is causing pain, because you will feel better one day and you have to let go to move on. While it reminds me how much

I can torture myself in a relationship that isn't making me happy, it also feels hopeful that you never know what is around the corner.'

'Heart of Glass' by Blondie (chosen by Justin Myers aka 'The Guyliner', author and columnist): 'This is one of the best breakup songs but is actually overlooked as one. Nobody seems to notice what it's about. Debbie Harry looking back with trademark indifference on the implosion of a relationship, thanks to a man who was a pain in the ass, is just perfect.'

'Without You' by Badfinger (chosen by Abigail Tarttelin, author): 'My mum was actually going out with a member of Badfinger at the time this was written. I think it's funny because it slightly annoys my otherwise unflappable dad, and also it's one of the saddest songs ever written.'

'Magic' by Coldplay (chosen by Kate Leaver, author): 'When I broke up with my boyfriend after seven years together, this had just come out. I think I played it on repeat for three months. It became the anthem for the breakdown of my relationship. I still can't listen to it without a little pang in my heart.'

'The Only' by Sasha Sloan (chosen by Kal Lavelle, singer-songwriter): 'Sasha is someone that really hits the nail on the head of sadness. She just knows how to express it in a real way and not a fake or generic way. "The Only" spoke to me because I was back on online dating after many years being out of the game. I was desperately trying to fill the void my ex left. And I was just thinking, "Jesus, am I the only one that feels so incredibly lonely." Because when you break up with someone, not only do you lose a lover but you lose your best friend… which is almost harder to deal with.'

'Distance' by AJJ (chosen by Matt Hoss, comedian and podcaster): 'This is an unconventional breakup song and it's pretty bold and out there, much like the rest of AJJ's work. But it's the most emotionally honest song about transitioning from being in a relationship. It's an honest depiction of a depressed single life. It is a sad song but it helped me massively to know that the pain is natural and it's a tough process. This song offers truth but also suggests that things do get better.'

'I'm Alive' by Jackson Browne (chosen by Zachary Stockill, podcaster): 'This song captures an often neglected aspect of breakup recovery – those moments when you blast your favourite song on the radio, wake up to see a new sunrise or you meet someone new…and you know in your gut that you are going to get through this pain, this loss. At the same time, you know that there will be more hard times, tears and moments of struggle. But interspersed throughout will be moments of grace when you know the breakup is for the best. Bigger and better things are on the horizon. "I'm Alive" expresses this post-breakup optimism perfectly.'

'Can't Breathe' by Tanya Stephens (chosen by Kate Smurthwaite, comedian): 'Female reggae voices are not that high profile. So the women that do emerge are super-tough in a way that you don't really get with your Adeles and your Western pop stars. In this song, there's a verse about seeing her ex looking happy with another woman. She puts all her vitriol into this verse, signing off with a hope that the woman leaves him for a girl. That's the moment that you do feel angry – when you see them with a new person and they're all happy and you're thinking, "Where's the arguing person that I had to deal with?"'

'Cold-Blooded Old Times' by Smog (chosen by Sarah Bennetto, comedian): 'This song is apposite because it's from Bill Callahan's Smog period, which people generally associate with his tumultuous "single" period. But his output during those lonesome dark days is phenomenal. Let's be clear…I'm not wishing misery on Mr Callaghan. But it gave the world this song. And for that we are thankful. It's a catchy, creepy little number about childhood memories and trauma. I promise you'll dance away the pain.'

'Remember' by Diana Ross (chosen by Vix Leyton, publicist and comedian): 'This is an absolute breakup anthem for when you reach the end of it, all the bitterness is gone and you just hope they take away something positive from your time together and remember you ultimately as a force for good in their lives, even if it wasn't meant to last. I think it's a lovely empowering song that allows me the space to be wistful but forward-looking.'

'This is the Day' by The The (chosen by Liz Bentley, comedian and psychotherapist): 'I think this song represents moving on in a literal sense for me. When I moved from Essex to London, it was on a compilation tape that my friend, later to become a boyfriend, had made for me. It continued to represent uplifting change and new horizons after each boyfriend split. I would play it with new boyfriends too. When I listen to it now, it brings tears to my eyes.'

'Jaa Chudail' by Suraj Jagan (chosen by Charvy Narain, science communicator): 'This is from the *Delhi Belly* soundtrack and is a fond homage to 1970s Bollywood. But I also like it because it's a petty revenge fantasy being dreamed up by someone who has just been dumped. So it's quite mean and angry. Which can be pretty cathartic.'

'You Haven't Seen the Last of Me' by Cher / 'Rise Like a Phoenix' by Conchita Wurst (chosen by Lena): 'The theme of both is of getting up after a fall and coming out as something better.'

'With or Without You' by U2 (chosen by Angie): 'This song makes me well up every time I hear it.'

'Keep on Movin'' by Five (chosen by Liz): 'I know it's a cheesy song but it's my bible for life.'

'Believe' by Cher (chosen by Zara): '"Believe" captures the thoughts I had immediately after my breakup, calling into question whether there really is life after love and the crushing soul-wrenching emotion of feeling lost and broken by grief, wondering whether the pain would ever shift into anything else.'

'Jealous' by Sinead O'Connor (chosen by Boozy Ex-Girlfriend): 'Whenever I hear it I'm taken back to the time when I'd first moved into my new flat after the fire. It was a stormy time for a little while after we'd broken up and you shared this song with me and I remember listening to it over and over.'

'Never Be Mine' by Kate Bush (chosen by Nice Ex-Girlfriend): 'It's a really comforting song about not ever getting together with someone and about being where you want to be, happy with a dream rather than a reality. It's quite unusual as pop songs go, which often follow a well-trodden "woe is me" narrative.'

'It's Time' by Imagine Dragons (chosen by Girlfriend): 'I had a pivotal moment when I listened to the lyric about not changing who you are and realised that, "for the right person, I'm enough."'

'You're The One' by Kate Bush (chosen by me): I used to wallow in this song when I first moved to London and was still infatuated with Older Ex-Girlfriend. I was frozen to the spot when I first heard the *Red Shoes* album on a listening post at Virgin Megastore on Oxford Street. I bought the album on cassette, which probably wore out after this song had been rewound and replayed so many times.

Bite-sized Breakup Stories

Maggy Whitehouse is a priest, comedian and author. Her ex-husband did a disappearing act after falling for a woman from New York. He flew out to be with her on 11 September 2001. She says, 'The first I knew of why or where he'd gone was when my mother-in-law phoned me in a panic to say she was afraid he'd gone into one of the Twin Towers. I was working at the BBC World Service that night and managed to find out that he had been diverted to Newfoundland, where he stayed for a week. So he didn't get to have sex with his new girl quite as soon as he'd hoped!'

Maggy's faith made it difficult for her to ask for a divorce. So she made him wait for two years until she could come to terms with 'giving the marriage back to God'. By that time, he'd broken up with the new woman anyway...then met someone else and got dumped. He had the cheek to phone Maggy to ask her advice about coping with rejection. Needless to say, he got short shrift.

Diane Spencer is a London-based comedian who began her career in New Zealand. While living over there, she broke up from a man that she believed to be 'the one' and started seeing someone else. There were many indications that this new love interest was not well suited to her 'jolly' persona. 'Even his penis was curved down – it was the most negative penis I've ever encountered,' she jokes. Nevertheless, she decided to turn up at his place in a sexy cowboy outfit one night. As he answered the door, she opened her trench coat to reveal her PVC chaps and said, 'Wanna have sex?' His response was, 'I'm just tuning my guitar.' Diane decided to leave him right then and there. 'I have these moments where I can see objectively and it's so much of a signal that it outweighs the drug impact of the love.' As she was driving back, she got stopped at a police breathalyser checkpoint. She was still in her cowboy hat and full costume. She confessed that she'd had one drink. The officer asked, 'Have you been to a party?' Diane replied, 'No. I'm just dressed as a cowboy.' To which he said, 'Well I'm dressed as a police officer' and let her go.

Back in the days of landline phones, Sarah Bennetto was dumped by her boyfriend's mother. 'I called to speak to Chris and she answered, saying, "Chris won't be coming to the phone." So I said, "Oh, OK, let me know when he's back" and she said, "Chris will never be coming to the phone." He was from an upper-class family and I was this working-class girl who'd put herself through uni. I'm not sure I was ever good enough. So as soon as she saw a tiny opportunity, she thought, "I'm going to revel in this." That was the vibe I got.'

Sarah had another strange breakup at school. While she and her friends were playing board games in the common room, they looked out of the window to see her ex sitting on the bleachers weeping and holding some pieces of paper. She says, 'I went outside with the entire school watching me. He passed me the pieces of paper. It turns out his four-year-old sister had drawn pictures of him, myself and her holding hands outside a house with a smiling sun shining down on us. That was a low blow.'

Comedian Elf Lyons experienced the sting of infidelity as a teenager when her friend took her to one side to say that her boyfriend of three months ('which is a full marriage in teenage years') had been 'fingering Marie in religious studies'. She informed said boyfriend that he'd have to make a grand gesture to win her back. So he did. He climbed up on a table in the school common room and serenaded her…with a performance of Sisqo's 'Thong Song'. Elf decided to re-evaluate her life choices.

When writer Abigail Tarttelin was living in LA, she broke up with her boyfriend after two and a half years together. 'He couldn't bear to watch me pack, so he headed out to a cafe to do some work. He could be a bit dramatic and he cycled off with big headphones on…and he got hit by a car. Because I was moving house, nobody could get hold of me until hours later. When I arrived at the hospital, the staff said, "We don't know whether he'll live or die…it's fifty-fifty." So I stayed for a month at the hospital with him. None of his family knew that we had broken up, and when he woke up he had amnesia and couldn't remember it. I could hardly argue with him when we were surrounded by people. We really nailed the recovery though…and it does make you closer when you get through something like that together. A couple of months later we did still break up. But he ultimately broke up with me when I said no to being in an open relationship.'

Meanwhile, actress Frances Barber once tried to prevent a big love of her life making a getaway…by running after him into the street and lying down naked in front of his car. The trouble was she lived in a cul-de-sac and everyone was looking out of the window. After he drove around her onto the pavement, she had to get up and walk back into the house. She laughs. 'I remember turning round and just saying, "I'm fine if anyone's interested."' She never spoke to the man again.

A Few of my Favourite Breakup Films

Appropriate Behaviour: This whip-smart comedy written and directed by the brilliant Desiree Akhavan, who I was once lucky enough to interview on the radio, follows Shirin, a bisexual Persian American woman in Brooklyn struggling to rebuild her life after breaking up with her girlfriend Maxine. As she drunkenly stumbles through awkward dates and threesomes and finally out of the closet, bittersweet flashbacks tell the story of the relationship.

Before Sunset: This seems an unlikely selection for a list of breakup films. The centrepiece of Richard Linklater's brilliantly naturalistic trilogy about love, in all its awkward humanity, sees Jesse and Céline actually get together. However, a beautiful scene on a boat trip through Paris sees the two characters, played by Ethan Hawke and Julie Delpy, sharing stories about Notre-Dame. Suddenly Céline breaks into a touching monologue about how people are so unique that they are not interchangeable. When something ends, it really is lost. That painful fact makes her hesitant to get involved. I am always reminded of my very early relationships and how I would sometimes ask, 'What's going to happen when we break up?' I shared Céline's fear that experiences and connections can be so very transient.

Blue is the Warmest Colour: Controversial I know. Most of my friends passionately hate this film. And it is, admittedly, problematic. Director Abdellatif Kechiche came under fire for cruel, exploitative treatment of his actors and crew, and for the overlong, inauthentic, soft-porny sex scenes (scissoring, anyone??). I first watched this in a tiny press screening room squashed in between male film critics. It felt super-odd to witness such a male packaging of lesbian sexuality and sex with a load of men. But, all that aside, the visceral breakup scene in the cafe is one of the most authentic depictions of the pain of rejection I have ever seen. Adèle Exarchopoulos is stunning in this scene, if a little snotty. Ugh.

Call Me by Your Name: This exquisitely filmed tale of awkward first lust and love in the heat of 1980s Italy ends with heartbroken teenager Elio sitting crying by the fireplace, the fragility of Sufjan Stevens' songwriting providing the perfect soundtrack. Just before this scene, Elio's wise father urges him to learn from his grief and grow, instead of just moving on too quickly.

Eternal Sunshine of the Spotless Mind: Full disclosure: I have a huge crush on Kate Winslet. So an oddball sci-fi romantic drama starring her is a huge win for me. And the premise of whether we would ever want to erase an ex from our memory is such a fascinating one...and, in the second half of this book, you'll discover that it is perhaps no longer a purely hypothetical one.

Her: Samantha, the conscious computer operating system voiced by Scarlett Johansson in this quirky and poetic Spike Jonze film, scours problem pages so that she can learn to be as complex as a human. She worries that her feelings aren't real but are just programming. Perhaps we should all worry about that. Eventually she evolves so quickly that she outstrips her introvert human lover, Theodore, brilliantly played by Joaquin Phoenix.

High Fidelity: In the year 2000, Nick Hornby's novel *High Fidelity* was adapted for the screen and explored disaffected record store owner Rob's need to compile and rank his top five breakups...and then bulldoze his way into a belated face-to-face post-mortem with each ex. While the music nerds of the original film are all a particular type of straight, white, self-obsessed man, unaware of the impact they may have on the women around them, a new TV adaptation places Zoë Kravitz[1] as a female 'Rob' (or Robin) and a coterie of women, queers and people of colour in the eternally customer-free shop. We can geek out about breakups, too. Yay!

Marriage Story: Scarlett Johansson (again!) and Adam Driver deftly portray two very relatable and very human people who have drifted apart through conflicting career needs. Their respective divorce lawyers then ramp up the discord until it explodes into a heartbreaking argument. The film's lineage traces back to 1979 Oscar-winner *Kramer vs Kramer*, which sensitively explored the impact of divorce on a child, single parenting and gender roles, rather than the slapstick plate-smashing of 1989's *The War of the Roses*.

Take This Waltz: At first glance, I thought this was going to be a breezy, sweet romantic drama. However, nothing directed by fiercely intelligent Canadian Sarah Polley and starring an actor as emotive as Michelle Williams is going to be a completely easy ride. The affecting punch is delivered towards the end by lead character Margot's alcoholic best friend Geraldine, played by Sarah Silverman. Perhaps changing partners isn't always the answer when we are in a slight pause in life. Perhaps we don't always have to fill it up with our chaos.

1 Daughter of Lisa Bonet who appeared in the 2000 original as singer-songwriter character Maria DeSalle.

Part Three
Forwards

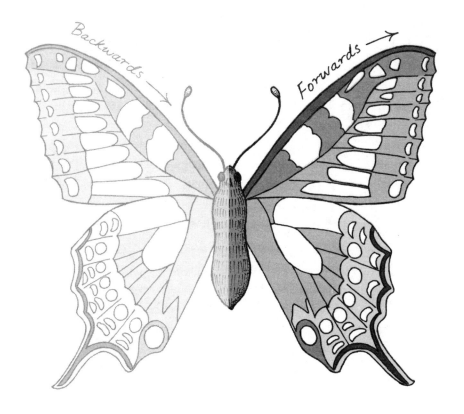

16

Beginnings are Endings and Endings are Beginnings

20 minutes B.G. (Before Girlfriend)

'My favourite days are the last ones of being single and the first ones of not being.'

I make a mental note of this to myself as I cross my beloved Brockwell Park, up past the tennis courts and the walled garden then downhill towards the Lido and Herne Hill. I peek in at the sun glinting on the water as a few hardy autumn swimmers splash up and down. I'm not heading for the pool today. I have a date.

These are happy times. Freedom is all the more exhilarating when you know that it may end soon. I should make the most of it. The thrill of flirtation, of constant messaging, has an altogether different level of security underpinning it this time. This time, I know she's interested. This time, it's happening. I walk taller, buoyed by this assurance. I haven't even thought about The Bisexual Comedian in days.

I have borrowed Nice Ex-Girlfriend's smart coat, one of a few cool things she hasn't yet picked up from the Brixton house. She knows I still wear her stuff and, generously, doesn't seem too perturbed by it.

I have an unfamiliar sexy swagger as I swoosh into Milk Wood, with its effortlessly trendy wooden tables, hipster staff and Laura Marling playing in the background.

My date is here already, smiling, with a pot of green tea.

'So…you do comedy?'

'Hmm yeah…I hope you haven't looked up any clips. There's some very old, random stuff on YouTube.'

'No…I haven't been very good at stalking.'

'That's good.'

It really is good. Even though I'm far from a household name, it's hard to date queer women in London who haven't been at some weird gig I've performed at sometime and therefore presupposed an ill-informed one-dimensional view of me. But she's not really involved with the scene. She's been in a closeted relationship for fifteen years. She's barely been to a queer bar, Pride festival or lesbian meetup. This is sexy. She is removed from the incestuous circles I normally move in. It doesn't feel so much like 'family'.

'And you work in…tennis?'

'Yeah, I help tennis players with their strength and conditioning.'

'I love tennis. I mean…I'm rubbish. But I love watching it.'

She regales me with all the gossip about the top players. It's immediately refreshing to talk about something other than queer politics, comedy or writing.[1]

Tea turns to wine. The conversation switches to her trek up the Andes and a recent holiday with her mum, who has just finished cancer treatment.

'Sitting by the pool all day and staying within the hotel complex for all our meals wasn't so much my usual kind of action holiday. But she needed to completely chill. I could go out for a run every day. So it was OK. It was lovely to spend time with her.'

I'm drawn to her authenticity and kindness.

We have a lingering hug at Herne Hill station.

---

1   It's perhaps also good that we don't dwell too much on past relationships. A friend recently got sent a list of dos and don'ts for a first date by a lesbian matchmaking company who had headhunted her as a potential date for one of their clients. She was strictly reminded to keep the conversation 'light'. 'Exes, health problems and dead pets' were on the banned list! Although they had worded it in a comically clunky way, perhaps they have a point. Lesbians love to talk about an ex. Sometimes they even bring them along to the date, as a sort of assessor.

I don't feel that overwhelming, explosive sense of need for more physical contact yet. There's just a positive secure feeling that she will be in touch and we will get together. This lack of an instantaneous mystical force field of attraction is a relief. I have learned the hard way that what sometimes feels like 'connection' can actually be old trauma reignited. Pain can feel familiar so we run towards more of it. Sometimes you've got to be kind to yourself and choose somebody different.

As I get older, I realise that all the classic stories of 'star-crossed lovers', far from being romantic, are desperately tragic. One or both usually end up dead or destitute. Psychologist and philosopher Erich Fromm once said, 'If love were only a feeling, there would be no basis for the promise to love each other forever.' I want someone reliable, who can actually keep a promise.

Without all of my bad breakups, without all the times I waited around for Agoraphobic Ex-Girlfriend, without all the times I wondered if Secretive Ex-Girlfriend was telling me the whole truth, without the myriad uncomfortable feelings that I *didn't* want, I wouldn't be in a position to know what I *do* want. I wouldn't be in a position to make this better choice. None of those relationships were supposed to last forever, yet a combination of them has brought me here…to a more alluring destination. Far from being failures at love, they might have been successes at learning. I hung around a little too long sometimes. But I still took the lesson away in the end.

When she appeared on the podcast, Pippa Evans likened the evolution of her partner choices to the famous 'evolution of man' drawing, first published as *The March of Progress* or *The Road to Homo Sapiens* in 1965, her husband represented by the upright 'modern man' and some of her earlier partner choices illustrated by the stooping apes. Although, interestingly, a 2019 study conducted at the University of Toronto's Psychology Department found that people's new partners tend to have a degree of similarity to their previous partners. Perhaps most of us really do have a 'type', even if we refine it and seek better versions of it as we go along.

As first dates go, mine with Girlfriend is really rather sweet compared to the hellish tales that my female comedy peers regale me with. Many are so bad that they break up there and then.

Ros Ballinger went to a fetish night where her date brought the two other members of his existing triad relationship. She would've been fine with this…except that he clearly hadn't told either that he'd invited someone else.

Jeanette Cousland's dinner date was so nervous that he set his sleeve on fire with the tea light on the table then fell off the chair dragging the tablecloth and table contents with him. He landed face down in a yucca plant. With his face covered in earth and chicken curry, staff poured water over him to extinguish the fire. She made her own slapstick exit, tripping over him as she tried to leave.

When she was eighteen, Angela Barnes met a guy who asked her on a date to a party he was having at 'his place'. It turned out to be his parents' house and their twenty-fifth wedding anniversary party. She had to wait until it was over for him to drive her home. Abi Symons tried to escape from a date through a toilet window but got stuck and her shoes fell off into the alley below. She had to sheepishly return to the dinner table barefoot. Meanwhile, Joy Harvey tried to excuse herself from a bad date by saying she had a tattoo appointment. He insisted on accompanying her. So she ended up getting an unwanted tattoo of Elvis.

A few days and many messages later, Girlfriend and I meet at Winter Wonderland[2] for mulled wine and mooching.

On greeting, she hands me a Waitrose flapjack, after having promised one of her home-baked ones.

'Yours didn't turn out so well, then?'

'They were gluten free…so just dust really.'

While she may have lost points on baking, at least she shops in a good supermarket.

As we exit the park, moving into a private blackness away from the glare of fairground lights, she begins an overly detailed account of a friend undergoing some psychometric tests.

'If you actually get to the end of this story, I'll give you a kiss.'

She doesn't reach the end of the story.

And the kiss is so magical that it's instantly very clear we are embarking on a new story that may also not end for a while.

---

2 A festive open-air Christmas market and fair held in London's Hyde Park every year with warming drinks, street food, music, ice skating and rollercoaster rides. To be honest, it was a slightly less classy date option than I realised when I suggested it.

17

A Fart in a Graveyard... and the Value of Arguing

5 months A.G. (After Girlfriend)

'Are we having a romantic few days away or am I just driving you around on tour?'

'Oh...erm...I think we're having a few days away and I just happen to be doing a gig during our break.'

'But you booked the gig before we booked the holiday.'

'Oh yes, that's true.'

We are driving to Salisbury[1] for their inaugural Queer Arts Weekender (or Squawk festival), where my solo show has been programmed at the beautiful Arts Centre, housed in the listed St Edmund's Church building, on an evening bill also featuring Northern folk duo O'Hooley and Tidow.[2] A good booking like this for a decent fee and in a space with all the proper tech support a performer can only dream of at Edinburgh Fringe always fills me with a happy sense of validation. Yet I am anxiously checking emails while sitting on the toilet at Fleet services. I'm in the midst of an Arts Council application

---

1 Pretty chilled Wiltshire city, later to become famous for being the location of the poisoning of a former Russian military officer/double agent and his daughter.
2 Later to become famous for their *Gentleman Jack* television theme tune.

for a new project, a storytelling and chat show called *The Breakup Monologues*.[3] Perhaps it might even be a podcast too. That seems to be the thing to do now if you're a comedian. But I need some venues to book the show in order for me to build a proposed tour schedule. I've got a commission from Bradford Literary Festival. But why has nobody else replied? Bastards.

'You were ages! Funny tummy? Or lots of emails?'

'Sorry.'

Girlfriend's car is loaded up with multipacks of Custard Creams and all manner of road trip snacks. The heated seats render a roof-down ride perfectly tolerable in early spring. Before checking into our B&B, we pop over to the Larmer Tree Gardens and wander among the peacocks and ornately painted outdoor stages, miniature temples and curious Victorian buildings. I reminisce about my past experiences at the End of the Road Festival held on the site and Girlfriend, naturally more curious about people, eavesdrops on a demanding 'bridezilla' touring her prospective wedding venue with her downtrodden parents. Opened to the public as the Larmer Tree Pleasure Grounds in the 1880s, the gardens were illuminated in the evenings and described by Thomas Hardy as the 'prettiest sight I ever saw in my life'. On this beautiful clear day, strolling through the rhododendrons with Girlfriend, they do hold a certain magic.

Our conversation turns to my potential imminent expulsion from my rented house in Brixton. Nice Ex-Girlfriend has allowed me to keep her name on the contract temporarily so that I can stay on. Yet the renewal date is looming. Girlfriend wants to buy a house and has put her flat on the market. But she doesn't want us to be pressured by the situation.

'I would hate us to rush into moving in together just because of money. I want us to do it because we love each other and it's right.'

That's easy for her to say. A comedian's income scarcely covers the council tax and bills, let alone the dreaded rent. Even with *Diva* magazine sponsoring my weekly radio show, things are incredibly tight now that I've got to pay for a whole place on my own.

---

3   Yes! The one that inspired this book.

'Yes, of course,' I sigh, knowing that it will be a little bit because of money as well.

After my show, we only have twenty-five minutes to get dinner before heading back in to hear O'Hooley and Tidow.

'They're friends who have booked me at cabaret nights over the years. I don't want to miss them. I know that doesn't really leave time for a lovely meal out. Sorry.'

'How about that chip shop up the road? It looked cute.'

As we ravenously tuck into fish and chips outside the venue, with the odd audience member walking past waving or smiling an acknowledgement, I inadvertently let a high-pitched but resonant fart escape.

'Oh, excuse me. I'm so sorry.'

'Baby! Not while we're eating. That's disgusting.'

'Honestly I didn't do it on purpose. It just slipped out. I'm really sorry'

'Don't ever fart again while we're having dinner.'

'We're eating chips in a graveyard. It's hardly candlelit dinner.'

'It doesn't matter. I'm eating.'

Girlfriend is genuinely upset. I'm tempted to laugh but know that this will aggravate things. So we sit in silence.[4]

'Now you're chewing noisily.'

Oh Christ. A few months in, I thought we were approaching the stage where we could start to breathe a little and stop having to act our best selves the entire time. This is sometimes known as the 'adjustment phase'. The thrill of the honeymoon period is subsiding and we are starting to see what the other person is really like. But we haven't yet reached the more established phase of deep companionship and longer-term commitment. It is still a danger zone. Many couples decide that it is easier to quit now before their lives get too entangled.

It's so exhausting to have to police one's behaviour 24/7, to hold back every involuntary eruption, to suppress our oddest tics. After a gig, I often need a moment of recovery time where I can just forget myself for a while, in a green room or backstage where I'm no longer under

---

4   Fart arguments are common, with many actually leading to breakups. Online threads on this include the headings 'Accidentally farted on my boyfriend and now he wants to break up' and 'my ex's constant farting led to our breakup.'

scrutiny. But with Girlfriend, I'm constantly under the fiercest spotlight of all. Nothing gets past her. Will I ever be able to relax again? Argh! It's *so* frustrating.

However, I need a life ally like Girlfriend. Although she calls me out on some of my peculiar habits, she gets it.

'I see you,' she said on several of our early dates. I had never been 'seen' before, not fully. Nice Ex-Girlfriend didn't seem to notice that I was strange. If she did, she just made a joke out of it. That didn't enable me to change and try to fit in better.

I always thought I was different because I was gay. But then I met hundreds of gay people and I was different to most of them too. Not in a life-altering way. But just enough to complicate a frustrating number of relationships, friendships and professional collaborations. I gradually became aware that my brain worked in a different way.

My forensic obsession with seemingly meaningless details, the near panic attacks brought on by choosing from a menu in a restaurant, the talking to myself, the uncanny ability to remember and recite a database full of personal email addresses…all these things were just weird until Girlfriend recognised it. She had an ex who was somewhere on a spectrum of what we now refer to as 'neurodiversity'. 'A little bit asparagus' is what we call it, because we like asparagus[5] and it sounds more fun than Asperger's. Anyway, I have more of a leaning towards it than a full-on condition. So in the absence of any official diagnosis, it makes sense. And for all the precarious tightrope-walking around one another's hormonal moods, short tempers and intolerances, Girlfriend and I make sense, too.

The next day we visit Stonehenge, buoyed by the fact that I've started getting some tour bookings in. Horrified at the near-twenty pound ticket price for a minibus up the road to stand at a rope cordon near the stones, we decide to walk up as close as we can instead. My frugality must be wearing off on her. All tensions dissolved, we have a wild and passionate snog in a small wooded area, the line 'Will you copse off with me?' making us giggle far more than it should.

Arguing with Girlfriend and being able to recover so quickly feels reassuring. I feel on a firm footing. Psychologist Dr Ed Tronick believes

---

5   Except for the way it makes your wee smell a few hours after eating it.

that rough patches and conflicts are crucial to our social and emotional development. By working through them, we build deeper, lasting connections. In his book *The Power of Discord*, co-written with Dr Claudia Gold, he says that, 'Misunderstandings are necessary to access the repair that provides energy for growth and change. When two people move from misunderstanding to understanding, they connect with each other.'

By contrast, when I was with Nice Ex-Girlfriend everything was just a bit *too* calm. It often spooked me. I knew she hated conflict because she witnessed it at close quarters as a teenager when her parents divorced. I couldn't ever fully know or share that experience, so I felt like an aggressive dick trying to push her into an argument. Meanwhile Girlfriend's ex would sometimes push her into arguing about their argument by questioning a particular word she had used. Whereas now that we are together, she avoids disappearing down a rabbit hole of meta-conflicts and I am liberated from my old hunger to actively pursue a fight. They just spark into life out of nowhere. And then they flicker away again, resolved.[6]

Out in nature, feeling happy and free, I wonder to myself...Now that I've found who and how I want to be in a romantic relationship, with someone who accepts me for all my annoying flaws, perhaps I can start to apply some of the lessons I've learned in order to ameliorate some of the stress and sadness that have begun to encroach on my professional life.

---

6 According to *Psychology Today*, 'Arguing can be very beneficial to the health of friendships and romantic relationships' so long as you remember four simple tips. Conflict should be seen as an opportunity to get to know one another better rather than as a threat. Second, it's important to recognise when you are ready to argue once the raw emotions have subsided. Third, we should be open to changing our minds rather than have a set expectation of how things should turn out. Finally, we need to recognise that our partner is just as vulnerable as we are.

18
The Professional Breakup

7 months A.G. (After Girlfriend)

'I just really need to get paid.'

'Writers don't get paid.'

This is the last thing that my first ever literary agent will ever say to me, her dismissive, withering shrug rendering it all the more cutting.

I am standing at the threshold of her office, fighting back tears, trying to push actual words out of my mouth. But no more will come. A strangled death rattle will have to suffice as a farewell. I reach out dizzily for the lift button, squashing and swallowing down the panic, praying that my carriage out of this hell arrives swiftly. Then I am out, free on the streets, disoriented by the abrupt hubbub of Brixton Road after the quiet bookish studio, my cheeks burning with indignation, the beginnings of a migraine singing in my ears. The warm city air makes a bellowing sound as I gasp and gulp it in, a peculiar accompaniment to a busker's stilted rendition of 'No Woman, No Cry'. I don't know who or where I am any more. I can't even remember how to get home.

How could this happen? To be told by an ally, one that I trusted so completely, that my work, and by default my entire existence, has no value…it's just too much to take in. My work, my performance…that stuff is the very fibre of me. It *is* me. I always took great pains to make it explicit that I could not afford to work for free. I'm a creative freelancer. Everything that I do has to bring in money for rent and bills. And ethically I refuse to work for free because it lets down all the other creative freelancers who are then, in turn, expected to work for free. She knows my position. I stated it again and again, as I invested more and more time and energy in researching and creating a book that she had advised me to write. We had made our plan *together*.

This was my opportunity to step up my game and become the entrepreneurial success that Girlfriend thought I was on our first date, when my wardrobe was largely borrowed from Nice Ex-Girlfriend. I'm all too aware that my grungy student outlook on life is not aspirational enough for my partner. There's a lot riding on this. I've unearthed a ton of speaking opportunities, way more lucrative than comedy gigs. But for those to happen, the book has to come out, get into shops, get reviewed and sell copies. And now I've got to make all that happen on my own. I feel excruciatingly lonely. The stress of writing a book and launching it into the world is like multiple Edinburgh Fringes all colliding together in a clusterfuck of rejection.

And now, on top of all that, I have been made to feel like a naive little girl by someone who sits in her office with her salary, her holiday and sick pay, while I stumble onto the street wondering how long I can survive on toast, cheese and Marmite.

Because we were friends before working together, it feels so much worse. She knows all about my constant struggle to stay afloat financially. How can she possibly *not* understand the catastrophic significance of not being paid? Perhaps most of the authors she knows have another job, savings, rich family networks, magic money trees in the back garden or some other way of covering their day-to-day costs.

Admittedly, we have been unlucky. A publisher going out of business was never part of our plan. It's never part of anyone's plan. But I didn't know that I would be made to feel like *I* was the crazy one, the 'difficult' author trying to save her livelihood.

It will take me three years to heal these scars and trust the publishing industry again,[1] equivalent to the longest ever time I have spent single. Maybe a professional breakup is just as traumatic as a romantic one.

Author Kate Leaver says, 'We don't give ourselves time and space to grieve when we're our work selves. We're meant to put decorum and dignity above everything else. But I think people need to be more open and vulnerable in the work space, which includes being upset when shit goes down between people we care about.'

Columnist, comedian and former Labour adviser Ayesha Hazarika agrees. As a child of immigrants growing up in Glasgow, she never felt like she 'fitted in' anywhere until she came to London and started working for the Labour Party. Suddenly, she had found her tribe and felt enveloped in a sense of 'it's not just a job, it's a cause'. She was so dedicated to this cause that she gave up her 'child-bearing years'. Her long-term relationship suffered and ultimately ended because her primary focus was the 'us against the world' energy that she discovered with her colleagues.

But then the Labour Party changed very rapidly in 2015 when Jeremy Corbyn won a leadership election. Ayesha thought she would continue to work for the party, despite the changes. Yet she found herself being dumped, along with many others.

Still sounding a little shaken by it, she says, 'I am still a Labour Party member. But I was thinking at the time, "How can this happen? I was working really, really hard and my ovaries have all shrivelled up now." It's one of those weird things…to have the thing that you love, your tribe, fracture is so discombobulating. These used to be my people. I don't mind being trolled by the far right. But I was even being trolled by a library! I found that emotionally really tough.'

---

1   I found an enthusiastic, super-cool agent and an empathetic, generous editor who didn't think I was a freak for wanting an advance to pay for things like electricity, gas and food. It worked out OK. Although I believe this is about more than just electricity bills. If we accept a system where one person is arbitrarily paid a vast amount while another is paid next to nothing for doing exactly the same job, it reinforces an uncomfortable social hierarchy which seeps into the rest of our lives. People are deemed 'better' and of higher worth if they have certain attributes like beauty or extroversion or are simply part of the straight white majority. Introverts, minorities and outsiders are effectively…dumped. Inclusivity isn't served by us paying lip service to it on a designated day on Twitter. It should be about equal pay. Put your money where your mouth is, as they say.

Comedian and coach Harriet Beveridge was 'delighted' to return to work after her second maternity leave in 2009. 'I remember getting a train to London and marvelling at the ninety minutes of peace. My clothes remained clean and vomit-free. I then spent an intoxicating day having real conversations with actual grownups.' But her confidence was low. Her company had merged while she was away so there were suddenly lots of people she didn't know. She had no idea because she hadn't been put on the email distribution list. 'Perhaps that should've been the first sign of alarm,' she says, 'like the first time a lover doesn't bother to text.'

After buying a new wardrobe full of post-baby work clothes and giving up breastfeeding so that she'd be ready for travel and meetings without leaking, she discovered that she was on the list for redundancy. A woman she had never met before abstractly talked her through how she 'scored' on her business acumen and contribution to the company, as if it was 'that bit in *Dangerous Liaisons* where the female character pleads and the cad's response is that it is beyond his control. Any argument I had was countered with a reference to the "process".'

Her husband, friends and fellow mums at the toddler group listened to her and helped her through the painful experience. Some swiftly offered up professional opportunities and possible collaborations. She kept working even if the money was tiny. 'It was a bit like flirting but not actively pursuing a relationship. I was freelance for about a year before I accepted employment. With hindsight, I can see that I didn't want to get burned again. Reminiscing a decade on, I can say hand on heart that I'm glad it happened. I learned who my real friends are, what resourcefulness I had and what opportunities I was missing. I think the key thing I took away is that whatever relationship we are in, there is something we all need to tap into: "This is who I am, this is what I have to offer and I'm worth being treated well."'

There are many parallels between a professional and personal breakup. The loss of an imagined future as a fabulous team still stings, particularly if you haven't been too long out of the 'honeymoon phase'. Likewise, the 'one that got away' feeling about the dream job we were shortlisted for but never got. Meanwhile, the awkwardness of working through a notice period can feel a lot like moving into the spare room for the final months of a co-tenancy rental contract (or working out who buys who out of a property you bought together).

Career coach Sara Young Wang has written about the loss of identity we feel when a job ends: 'Our minds tend to be constantly searching for labels to grasp onto and form a sense of self. They provide a sense of security and safety to know where we stand in the world. They allow us to project our future with the assumption that if this is who I am it will be lasting. This is reflected in our language. We say "I am" a banker, lawyer, wife, husband and so on. When asked to introduce oneself, it's expected that we will list off the labels. When we lose our job or experience a relationship breakup, we lose those labels.'

Yet, as with romantic endings, adversity can help us to make better choices and gain clarity about what we do want. We can transform it into an opportunity. Sara says, 'Success is getting to live a life you enjoy. The creation of that life is dependent on making choices that are in alignment with who you are. But that's not easy to do. We can often find ourselves in a situation where we have abandoned what we know to be right for us for what we think we *should* do – jobs we hate but look good on paper, relationships that don't feel right deep down but seem to make sense on the surface. This brings suffering. And that suffering is where we can learn a lot, find the courage to overcome those shoulds and pursue what we truly want.'

Perhaps my mistake was to cross over personal friendship with professional collaboration. Perhaps that is too muddy. Says Sara, 'If you are friends, it can be surprising when a professional dispute occurs. There was most likely a subconscious expectation that things would go smoothly. And the loss of the professional relationship feels greater as overall that person is more meaningful to you.'

A few weeks after the breakup with my agent, Girlfriend and I are at queer arts gathering LFest. My solo show gets several rounds of spontaneous applause after every storytelling section. Then my reading in the literary tent stirs everyone up into a boisterous hysteria quite unexpected on a festival Sunday morning, Becky and Lena among the familiar laughing and smiling faces. I love performing to my community, my family. Nothing beats it. Girlfriend and I run a makeshift book stall at the back of the venue after the show and sell dozens within a few minutes. Spontaneously, we slip into a slick system. She takes the money and I sign books. We are team mates. I feel like she's totally on my side. Once we've sold out the entire box, we jubilantly skip across the park to the main stage. 'Thanks for your help working out all the money. I could've never managed that queue on my own.' As a few beads of drizzle start to dampen and squash down her bouncy hair, she beams at me and says, 'I'm proud of you. You've written a brilliant book.'

If she believes in me, that's the main thing I need. I can just keep on searching for the right professional collaborators. I've just got to be accepting of what has happened with my agent, once I've had some time to heal.

We spend the rest of the evening sheltering from the downpour in a stables building which has been designated the artists' 'Green Room'. Becky and Lena run in, shivering and completely drenched from head to foot. They are camping but, true to form, haven't brought any waterproofs. Girlfriend points them to a big urn of hot tea, yet they opt for a jug of potent alcoholic punch instead. It's warming in a different way I suppose. I wonder what will happen to their relationship if either one of them ever decides to sober up enough to think about whether they're happy on a deeper level.

Watching them frenetically dancing themselves dry, I say to Girlfriend, 'Can we have a really chilled out holiday this year?'

19

Shared Values and Experiences

9 months A.G. (After Girlfriend)

'How have we managed to get things so right this time around after we messed up in the past? Did we learn from our breakups?'

We are sitting in the evening sun sharing a takeaway Four Seasons pizza on the balcony at a Spanish apartment belonging to our friends Jac and Ange. The sea sparkles on the horizon, the beach overlooked by the traditional whitewashed Moorish old town. After a stressful summer of poor health, the painful fallout with my agent and a disappointing Edinburgh, not to mention the misery of another Tory general election win, a week of lazing around, cuddling, talking, reading, swimming and eating huge slices of watermelon stretches out before me luxuriously. I need recovery time. And, for once, so does Girlfriend. Even her energies are drained by fitting her work around back-to-back festivals. This is the perfect time to reflect on our connection and how, in our own peculiar way, we have struck gold. We heal quickly from arguments, we don't harbour resentments. Somehow our funny old connection just works, despite our differences.

'The worst relationship of my life has led me to the best relationship of my life,' posits Girlfriend.

'Aww, baby.'

'In my previous relationship I was so compromised. I couldn't articulate my values and needs, so I was left feeling constantly disappointed. I couldn't do that again. When I met you, I was fine with being single. I had rediscovered myself and thought "This is me, this is alright. If I meet the right person it'll be enough. I'm not changing." I didn't go into us trying to be somebody for you. I think I was annoyingly boundaried, as in "This is it, take it or leave it." And I think maybe I've got more relaxed since then.'

Thinking about my 'forty love rule' I ask, 'Sometimes we say it's a shame we didn't meet sooner in life. But maybe we would've messed it up if we did. Did we need to learn from those past relationships? Did you need to find yourself and find out that you were fine with being single, do you reckon?'

Girlfriend looks at me, squinting in the sun, and states with certainty, 'If we'd met when we were younger, we wouldn't have got together.'

'Really...?' I say, a tiny bit crestfallen at how definite this is.

'I was living in a very small world in my head. Everything was about sport. You were arty, musical, cool and a lesbian activist. None of that was me. I was spending most of my time with my straight friends, busy being a tennis coach. I don't think we would've had a lot in common. I don't think we do now. But it doesn't matter now.'

'How do you mean? Is it just because we're older and we don't go out and do as much?'

'Even though our interests are different, our values are similar.'

'You mean like both voting to stay in Europe?'[1]

'Well yes, things like that. But also, I've changed so much since I was younger. I am already a person now. You add to that. Your way of being expands me. But I'm OK with me to start off with.'

'I'm pretty OK with you, too, sweetie. How do I expand you?'

---

1 In the few years leading up to the 'Brexit' referendum in the UK, there had been a decline in divorce rates. However, in its aftermath, this figure rose again. Couples were divided by this incredibly binary question. Our response to it seemed to say so much about our personal values, our sense of inclusivity. Hitherto unseen aspects of people were revealed, aspects that carry more resonance than superficial tastes in films or music. Partners who wanted to stay in the European Union felt deeply hurt and betrayed by partners who had voted to leave. It felt, to them, like their soulmates had all had an affair with Nigel Farage. Ugh! Similarly in the US, a 2017 poll found that 11 per cent of Americans ended a serious relationship due to political tensions in the wake of Donald Trump's election over Hillary Clinton. Forty-one per cent said that they argued with their partner over politics more than ever. Newspaper articles ran with headlines such as 'Donald Trump is Destroying my Marriage', 'If You Are Married to a Trump Supporter, Divorce Them' and 'I Might Still Be Married if Trump Wasn't President'. According to matchmakers and dating agencies, late 2016 was the first time that politics became one of the major criteria in people's searches. They wanted a partner who would be on their side.

'I was a right dick when I met you. Silly things mattered. I wouldn't go to Waitrose without my makeup on.'

'And now we go to Tesco looking like we've just mucked the horses out!'

'Hang on a minute. We've got to draw the line somewhere!'

'Haha…so have you ever thought that we would break up?'

'Just once.'

'At the station when we missed the train that time?'

'Yes. I didn't know you very well then. I had fallen completely in love with you. But I didn't really know who you were.'

'And you suddenly thought, "What the fuck? Who is this swearing idiot?"'

'Something like that.'

'I read recently about the idea of "flooding". I think it's a sort of reflex that circumvents logical thinking. You can suddenly go from relaxed to furious, seemingly for no reason. It can happen when you're on high alert, which I guess I can be after I come offstage. It hasn't often happened but that's what that experience felt like.'

'Interesting.'

'Maybe the new relationship was also a factor in a way. I was excited and on a high. But I was also stressed because I didn't fully know you yet either…Whereas now I just have this calm feeling most of the time. It's quite new for me. People can't hurt me in the same way now because you've got my back.'

'I've got you, baby.'

As I drift off to sleep, gazing at the hypnotic rotations of the ceiling fan, I think about how breakups, while they may hurt at the time, really do shape us in good ways and equip us to make much better choices.

The next morning, one of our neighbours, a tanned local man, walks across the shared courtyard towards the little oval pool as we are opening up the balcony doors.

'*Buenos días*,' he shouts up, smiling from under the brim of his straw hat.

Girlfriend leans on the balcony rail confidently and shouts back, '*Buenos Aires!*'

I do a double-take. Did she just say what I thought she said? She seemed so sure of herself. Surely not. I won't say anything.

The man, nodding and still beaming, walks on.

After an al fresco breakfast of nectarines and fresh, fluffy bread, we walk down the steep, quiet road towards the beach.

'Coming back up this isn't going to be fun! I hope we haven't forgotten anything,' shouts Girlfriend after me as I break into a jog ahead of her, desperate to get into the sea. 'I think I'll look into hiring a car.'

'Whatever you reckon, baby.'

Once we walk briskly across the hot sand and settle onto some recliners under umbrellas, we take off our T-shirts ready to go for a swim.

A man on the plane did warn us about the sea at Mojácar. 'It's very rough in the mornings,' he said sternly.

But it looks fine. A few waves crash up the beach and tickle our toes. Girlfriend steps forward until the water is up to her middle. I follow. Then the floor suddenly disappears from under me and I am somersaulting around inside a washing machine, pebbles and grit forcing their way up my nose and into every orifice. This is it. I'm dying. Which way up am I?

Then I am spat out again onto the beach further up than where I started. My carefully tied, elegant little ponytail has moved around to almost the front of my head. Mud seems to be pouring down my face. I pat my body down to check I'm still wearing both parts of my bikini. Girlfriend is laughing hysterically.

'Oh my god… Look at you!'

'What just happened?'

'A wave caught us. There's a sort of shelf where the water breaks and, if you don't get past it quickly, well…'

'You nearly drown??'

'Haha, something like that. Come on let's get showered over there. We'll feel better.'

'I think I'm still in shock.'

At the dribbly beach shower, I attempt to hose out grit from my bikini bottoms in the least revealing way possible. Finally clean and a bit more refreshed, we buy a cold beer from the beachside bar.

Feeling the fuzzy effects of the alcohol immediately, I venture, 'You know this morning when that man from one of the apartments said *buenos días*…?'

'Yes?'

'Did you say *Buenos Aires* back to him?'

'Oh bloody hell, did I? What a knob!'

A recent study of over 11,000 couples found that in-jokes and shared experiences, like perhaps making hapless attempts at foreign languages or getting humiliatingly 'washing-machined' in an unexpectedly vicious sea, are a vital part of the dynamic that you build with someone.[2] And that, in turn, is so much more important than the characteristics of the two separate individuals in terms of predicting relationship quality and satisfaction. So next time someone says to you, 'It's not you, it's me', you can call them out on it. Because science suggests it is *neither* of you. It's the dynamic between you.

Giggling our way through the week, we rest and repair our weary, dented souls. One afternoon a message arrives from my contact at the Arts Council to alert me to the news that I have received funding for the pilot stages of *The Breakup Monologues*. My financial woes are temporarily abated now that I have an exciting new project to work on. I don't think about the breakup with my agent at all. We even conquer the unpredictable wilful sea once we hire that car and make our way to another calmer section of beach.

Sitting on our towels on the warm sand one late afternoon, she says, 'Baby, can we start looking for a puppy when we get home?'

'Awww, oh my god, yes! How cute.'

'Oh yay! I can't wait to be a dog mummy with you.'

---

2   Survey conducted by Relationships Decision Lab and published in *Proceedings of the National Academy of Sciences*.

20

'Til Dog Us Do Part

Breakup Stories: Carly Smallman

When comedian Carly Smallman moved in her with her boyfriend after being together for a year, he was constantly 'banging on and on about getting a dog'. His family had three Jack Russell dogs that he was obsessed with. Carly was more cautious about this commitment, wondering what might happen to their new baby if they were ever to break up.

But when he kept on talking about it, she went and bought a cute puppy and surprised him. They had a lovely time together enjoying their new doggy life for the next six months. 'I thought we had it made,' she laughs. 'We lived in a Victorian conversion flat and shopped in Waitrose…like fucking winners! I thought we were happy.'

But then, as Christmas approached, Carly was summoned into the living room for a chat as she returned from buying decorations for the home she was so excited to be sharing with her boyfriend.

'I'm just not feeling this.'

'Why? What's wrong?'

'I don't want to talk about it. I'm just not feeling it.'

And that was that.

Carly called her mum and then gathered her belongings in a speedy 'smash and grab': 'You have to get all your stuff but, when you're in that state, it doesn't matter what stuff. I remember, in my grief, packing a swimming costume and a dressing gown.'

So a few days later her mum politely suggested that she might need to go back and collect some actual clothes. When she did, her dog Indie was there, clearly having been left alone for hours, surrounded by an empty water bowl and puddles of wee on the floor. So she took him.

Her ex phoned her much later when he returned from a long day at work.

'Thanks so much for taking the dog. I didn't want him any more. He's yours now.'

Carly thinks that she'd have been 'totally screwed' if she wasn't self-employed. Her comedy career gave her the flexibility to keep her new best friend. And that new best friend vastly improved her newly single social life: 'It did help me when I moved into my new flat because having a dog makes you make friends with your neighbours. When you're single, self-employed and live alone you can end up wondering if you'll go through a day without speaking to a soul. But when you have a dog, you end up speaking to everyone. I don't know what I'd do without him.'

When it comes to divorce law in many countries, including the UK, our beloved pets are viewed as pieces of property like a car or a stereo whose fate is decided without their welfare necessarily being taken into consideration. In 2017, Alaska became the first US state in which judges are required to treat animals more like children.[1] If Girlfriend and I were ever to separate, I'd be pretty likely to hang onto my feline 'fur-child'. She finds Cat beautiful in the same, slightly terrified way that she finds tigers and panthers beautiful.

Therefore I imagine that a dog will seem a bit like Girlfriend's baby. It's her thing. I'm just as clueless about dogs as she is about cats. But when I hear friends like Carly talking so positively about their doggy experiences, I think that maybe, just maybe, it might be good for me to open my mind to the canine world.

---

1   California and Illinois followed suit. When it comes to deciding who gets the pet, the judge must consider not just who paid for an animal, but who walks, feeds and plays with them and who takes them to the vet. Famous pet custody cases include that of Britney Spears, who was deemed 'unfit' to parent her Yorkie London even though she makes way more money than ex-husband Kevin Federline. Being named by PETA as the World's Worst Celebrity Dog Owner probably didn't help. When a partner enters a relationship with an existing pet, as I did with Cat, it is usually assumed that person is the owner. Drew Barrymore got to keep her Labrador Flossie after a legal showdown with her ex because she was the original owner.

These are the thoughts running through my head as we sit impatiently in traffic en route to a breeder in Norfolk to view an accidental litter of bockers[2] that we have seen online. There's one with a little brown and white face that we have fallen in love with. Our sat nav informed us it would be a ninety-minute drive. However, ninety minutes has turned into three hours. We were going to just go and have a look and then maybe come back another day to actually take the puppy home. But given how long it's taking, it feels like today or never.

We arrive hot and tired at a weird tumbledown farmhouse full of barefoot feral children merrily dancing in dog wee. We forget all the sensible questions we were supposed to ask, like 'Can we see the mother and father of the litter and check how healthy they are?' Instead, we just want to get our beautiful new puppy out of here. Although we think we can describe the one we want, a gruff woman brings the whole litter into the tatty living room. Girlfriend lies on the floor and the boy puppies all jump on her, licking her face and untying the shoelaces of her Converse sneakers. I pick up the little girl that we like.

'This one is lovely.'

'Yeah, she's cute. I'm sure she'll grow out of that underbite.'

'Oh, I hadn't noticed that.'

The other little girl puppy stumbles determinedly towards me. She has a completely brown face, huge ears and a white streak on her chest. I pick her up and she falls asleep in my arms. I don't want to move. Ever. She is adorable. It feels like she has chosen me.

Now I'm not sure what to do.

I look at Girlfriend and shrug to indicate my indecision.

'Can we pop out for a bit to discuss it and then come back?' she asks. 'We are starving and really need a bite to eat if there's a pub nearby?'

'Yes, there's one just down the road.'

As soon as we get back into the car, Girlfriend puts Glenda on speaker phone.

'Mam, we need your advice. We've seen a litter of puppies and we really love two of them.'

'Get both, love.'

---

2   As it's not really an official designer breed, there's no proper name for a beagle/cocker mix. We prefer 'beacock'.

'We can't. We have a cat and it's going to be too much to have two dogs suddenly running around.'

'Oh, OK, there we are then.'

Gorging on fish and chips, we decide it has to be the little one who came and chose me. Cradling her in my arms in the car home, she feels no bigger than the Snoopy toy I had as a child. I feel a rush of excitement but a little shiver of terror as well. What the hell have we just done?

The following week, Girlfriend buys a picture, gets it framed and hangs it on the wall. It's a cute cartoon drawing with two stick women, with curly and straight-ish hair respectively, a little brown dog and a tabby cat with triangular ears and a curling, wiggly tail. Above the drawing, the title reads, 'Our little family'.

21

We Are Family

1 year 7 months A.G. (After Girlfriend)

'Do you ever wish you'd had children?'

'Not so much now. But in my thirties, I felt this really desperate ache for a baby. But I wasn't in a secure relationship, or a secure financial position, or a secure anything really. Sometimes I cried when I got my period because I wasn't pregnant. I'm not sure how I was expecting it to happen. I used to do a slightly menacing routine about hoodwinking male comedians into giving me their sperm. That's how desperate I was. I was even considering male comics as unsuspecting donors.'

'Aw, baby.'

'Like I say, it's passed now though. Why...do *you* want children?'

'Not now, no. I might've if things had been different.'

'If you hadn't been gay?'

'Yeah...Anyway...I'm not gay, haha. What are you talking about?'

'Yeah yeah, you big lezzer.'

We are sitting with Dog in the idyllic grounds of the Wilderness rural estate in Suffolk, where we are residing for a three-day extravaganza to celebrate Girlfriend's brother's wedding. Watching her young nephew Jake playing football with some older boys, our conversation has turned to the notion of family and what it means for us. It strikes me that living through three decades of homophobia during those crucial fertile decades, our teens, twenties and thirties, has irreversibly altered the directions of our lives in ways that no amount of current social acceptance can undo. In our mid-forties, we are OK with not being parents. But it's quite a headfuck to think that the main reason for our childlessness is that we are gay and haven't been allowed to breed.

We simply haven't had access to the conventional structures of marriage and biological family that straight people take for granted. Professor of psychology at the University of Colorado, Scott Stanley, talks about a 'zone of ambiguity' that contemporary young people conduct their relationships within, now that people tend to marry and commit much later. This was, until recently, a permanent zone for gay people. Maybe we grew to enjoy the freedom of this zone, and the opportunity that it presented for the greater sexual variety of serial monogamy or the subversive thrill of open relationships. But who knows what would have happened if we'd had a choice.[1]

Perhaps, however, that choice can very easily feel more like a huge pressure. Rachel Creeger is the only practising Orthodox Jewish woman currently on the UK comedy circuit and is occasionally billed in the press as a 'real-life Mrs Maisel'. 'In our culture it's not the norm to date casually,' she says. 'Theoretically you are always dating with a view to marriage. It's common to get engaged after a few months.' So, many years ago, when a boy three years her senior started picking her up from school in his bright yellow sports car, it wasn't long before he started to drop hints that she should cancel her planned gap year in Israel and settle down, marry and start a family with him instead. One day he even swapped the garish two-seater for a family car, one that would apparently be more suitable for their children. Rachel was only eighteen and knew she wasn't ready. She felt so suffocated that she eventually screamed at him in the street and asked him not to contact her until she returned from her year away.

For six months, she had a blissful 'transformative' time with her kibbutz family. She received a letter from her ex telling her that he was seeing someone else. She was incredibly relieved to have some closure.

Yet one morning, she was summoned urgently away from work: 'I assumed that a close family member had died or been injured. I ran to my adoptive family's house and when I pushed the door open, I was shocked to see my ex sitting there drinking tea with them. He told me that he had signed up as a volunteer on the kibbutz for three months and that this proved how much he loved me. He said that the other relationship wasn't serious and that I owed it to him to see if we could work things

---

1 My comedian friend Debra-Jane Appelby had no choice *but* to get divorced when she underwent gender reassignment treatment in 1994. She was assigned a male identity at birth and was living as male when she married her wife. Prior to the 2004 UK Gender Recognition Act, there was no option for conversion to a civil partnership – as they didn't exist yet!

out. However, the separation had made me strong enough to see that this wouldn't be right for me and to tell him so.' Eventually she gathered some friends around her to back her up as she asked him to leave.

When she returned to the UK, relaxed and happy, she started dating her now husband Mark, an old friend from the local community: 'He is completely different to my ex, incredibly supportive and has never tried to change me in any way.' Even her ex was being friendly and apologetic now that they worked together at the same youth centre. One day he offered her a lift home. Rachel assumed that enough time had passed for it to be harmless. However, he took a different route, pulled into a side road, tried to kiss her and persuade her not to get married. Rachel ran to the nearest phone box and called her dad to ask him to pick her up.

Twenty-seven years later, she and Mark are happily married with two children. She only very occasionally bumps into her ex in the shops or in the street. If he tries to reminisce about their 'golden memories', she now finds it a bit 'pathetic' although at the time it was 'very disturbing'.

Broadcaster Remona Aly similarly had to call off a serious early romance before legally binding herself to someone who turned out not to be quite the right one. Speaking on *The Wintering Sessions* podcast, she recalls how excited she was to meet her former fiancé at a political demonstration, outside of the expected cultural setting of 'awkward samosas and tea' with a suitor and his entire family. A 'good muslim girl', she hadn't had any relationships while growing up and spent many a school disco 'sitting on the sidelines'. Yet she thought her new boyfriend was perfect. However, as time went on, alarm bells started to ring. Just before a huge engagement party, she had a panic attack: 'There was something in my gut telling me, "Do not do this."' But she felt such a sense of responsibility because her entire community were so invested in the forthcoming marriage. Although she went through with the celebrations, complete with a marquee, cake and a throng of excited relatives, she realised that she simply had to end the relationship. She feels that she had 'fallen into the gaps of someone else' and didn't recognise herself. She clung to her faith and her family, her dad supporting her by writing letters to all the family members to let them know that the wedding was off. She says, 'The first time I smiled again was three months later.' However, she reflects now that diving so deep into her emotions enabled her to understand herself better.

Rachel's and Remona's stories interest me because their early experiences are almost a polar opposite of mine. I assumed as a young lesbian emerging into the world that I would only ever be able to date casually and never have a relationship formally or legally recognised. So, to some extent, I wasn't sure it really mattered who I chose. Nothing would last forever anyway. Whereas they both had to demonstrate real strength of mind and character not to be swept up into long-term commitment before they were ready.

Do any of us really have an extravagance of options so freely and easily available to us, after all? Perhaps we are all equally constrained by the societal scripts that have been attached to love.

That said, I find it a bit tedious when straight people play a sort of breakup version of the card game Top Trumps. Once I met a woman who, when I told her about my podcast, said, 'Of course *my* breakup was a div-*orce*'. She placed an emphasis on that second syllable as if that underlined a greater significance than just a routine breakup. There was no hint of irony or awareness of the privilege attached to having been able to get married in the first place. I can understand that the legalities of paperwork, having to find 'reasons'[2] and waiting for the divorce to come through all add to the horrific stress of it. And then there's the question of what to do with all the wedding paraphernalia. Should there be a ritualistic dress burning? Should the engagement ring be melted down and fashioned into another piece of jewellery? And when that's all sorted, what about throwing a divorce party?[3]

But really…that stuff is just admin.[4] Married or not, the pain of a significant breakup is the same in my opinion. We all have that moment of sitting crying on a cold hard floor wondering if we will ever get up

---

2   Apparently having another relationship while separated counts as adultery even if nobody cheated while the couple were together. So even some amicable couples agree to cite adultery as a reason as a way to get things done quicker.

3   A friend of mine did have a party. He says, 'I got confirmation of my divorce via email as I was leaving the house to go to work. I wasn't expecting a fanfare and grand proclamation. But after the ceremony of a wedding, and then going through the archaic system of divorcing, it felt hugely anticlimactic. I wanted to mark this important moment with more significance.' So he organised drinks and dinner with a dozen close friends and family and asked his groomswoman to collate a book of messages, art, well-wishes and support. He found it incredibly cathartic.

4   Perhaps this admin won't be necessary for future generations. A 2018 poll for the Coalition for Marriage revealed that a quarter of 18- to 24-year-olds believed that marriage contracts should work like mobile phone contracts with a renewal date every couple of years.

again. For some reason, it is always the kitchen floor, the coldest, hardest one of all. We must really want to torture ourselves.

My belief is that heartbreak is the one thing that truly unites us across all sexualities. My relationships with Boozy Ex-Girlfriend, Secretive Ex-Girlfriend and Nice Ex-Girlfriend all lasted five years. Each was the equivalent of a marriage in my mind. In fact, Boozy Ex-Girlfriend did propose. But at the tail end of the 1990s, there was no legal option available to us.

Even my troubled union with Agoraphobic Ex-Girlfriend was hugely significant. Although it only lasted just over two years, we would most likely have progressed to the beta-endorphin phase described by Anna Machin. We were still plunged into opiate withdrawal. And even breakups after a very short time can hurt if we've attached an important psychological script to that potential future, as I had with The Bisexual Comedian.

Nowadays, of course, Girlfriend and I *could* get married. As we collapse into the voluptuous outdoor sofas, she taps me on the arm with a recent addition to our code. Tap tap tap-tap tap. 'Will you marry me?' I nod and wink. We love proposing just for shits and giggles...and where better than at an actual wedding?

But what about when one of us wants to do it for real? When you're both women, who asks who? What is the protocol? And what the hell do we wear? I would most likely opt for a dress, while she's more comfortable in a funky jumpsuit. But does that cement some kind of unrepresentative butch-femme dynamic in people's minds? And if we go casual, does that diminish the seriousness of the vows? I wish it wasn't so complex because I would really like to marry her. When someone is your best friend that you absolutely love and trust, then why the hell not?

I don't know where all this hesitancy and squeamishness about it comes from. Is it our own internalised shame? It's certainly not from our parents. Glenda comes to stay with us and happily sits in her dressing gown and pink slippers drinking tea from our Pride mug and asking Siri questions about LGBT history. Meanwhile, Dad always introduces Girlfriend as my 'paaartner' in a very deliberate comically elongated way if we bump into his neighbours and friends when we go and stay with him.

Legally bound or not, I feel wholeheartedly welcomed into Girlfriend's generous and loving family. With the main business of the actual wedding done and dusted, there remains the matter of a highly competitive treasure hunt. Girlfriend and I are teamed with her middle brother Paul and his brood. A soft-hearted ACDC fan who always sounds a bit pissed even when he's totally sober, he's the polar opposite of the groom, affluent career-driven eldest brother Dale.

'Right come on, Rosie, what have we got to do?' drawls Paul, browsing an extensive booklet full of complex tasks. Girlfriend and her niece Erin hop onto some old-school bikes with baskets on the front to scout out a hidden easel from which to paint a landscape of the estate. Then they will go and count jars of sweets at the shop near to the grounds entrance. The rest of us busy ourselves with shooting an impromptu music video and then skip down into a secluded winding spiral hollow to the oval-shaped swimming pool to film Jake jumping in and out of the water.

'It's nearly midday. If we run over to the lake now, we can do a bonus challenge.'

Girlfriend has also remembered the rule about the waterside on-the-hour rendezvous. She takes charge, teaming up with Paul to thrash Dale and his eldest son in a rowing race. Elated, we run back to the house where Glenda and her sister, Auntie Jan, sit drinking tea.

'They're very excited to have beaten Dale.'

'Oh well that's sibling rivalry, see.'

The next task is to create a 'table decoration' in one of the fancy rooms. Unimpressed by the few remaining sad fir cones and prim doilies left over by the other teams, Paul says, 'I'll give them a table decoration.' He strips naked and poses for a photo Adonis-like on the elegant long table with only a strategically placed silver tankard for decency. He's hardly the most lithe male specimen, bless him. Girlfriend has never seen me laugh so hard. Our team get bonus points for lateral thinking but miss out on the overall score by a fine margin to…Dale's team. Damn.[5]

A decade on from the rejection I felt at never being introduced to Secretive Ex-Girlfriend's parents, this inclusion in the joyful camaraderie of Girlfriend's extended family is all the sweeter. As we watch one of Dale's two huge strapping teenage sons from his first marriage bend down to pick up the tiny daughter from his third, it makes sense to me why, even in the face of divorce, people would want to make a huge effort to keep all their loved ones together in some way.

---

5   I'm as caught up in the sibling rivalry as everyone else.

22

Keeping it Together, Moving On

Breakup Stories: Wendy Wason

'My mum had two very acrimonious divorces so I was very mindful that I didn't want to put my kids through that.'

Comedian Wendy Wason's son and daughter were aged three and five when her marriage ended. At first, they were told that everything was fine and that Mummy and Daddy were just not living together any more. However, when a friend of Wendy's was babysitting while she was out doing a gig, the children started asking more questions. So Wendy and her ex sat them down for a chat.

Although Wendy gets on fine with her ex now, she describes feeling like she was 'on her knees' in the aftermath of the separation. She was a single mum, going out gigging, 'keeping it all together and looking after the children'. One month her ex said he had no money: 'I still had to find it because bills still have to be paid. The buck stops with you. But I had to decide not to be bitter about it because I didn't want my kids to see that.

'Now the kids are older, my ex wants to see them a lot more because teenagers are easier to take out for dinner. Younger kids need to be got up in the morning, fed, dressed and have their teeth brushed. So I have had moments of thinking, "So *now* you want them." But you've got to park all that stuff because you can start to feel really angry about it and it's not the kids' fault.'

Beginning a new relationship opened up as a possibility when she said to herself, "You know what. You're thirty-five. You've got two kids. You're lucky. Be grateful for what you've got. You were in love and now you're not. Just get on with it."

Soon afterwards she went out for lunch with fellow comedian Phil Nichol who advised her, 'You need to get back on the horse. You need to have a one-night stand. Have you ever had a one-night stand?' So she had her first ever one-night stand…and that has now lasted for over a decade!

She tried to warn off her new partner Stephen by saying, 'I'm the walking wounded. This is a fling. I want to go out drinking with you, we're going to have sex and it's going to be great. I don't want to have a relationship.' It turns out, apparently, that this is 'catnip' to men.

When Stephen was first introduced to the children, Wendy's son was delighted to have a new buddy, but Wendy's daughter 'put him through the mill for a good couple of months and was very defensive of her daddy.' But now they're all very close.

As we now live much longer than our ancestors, our long-term relationships are bound to struggle to meet our needs over such an expanse of time. Perhaps one marriage for life has become unrealistic. Added to that, a huge shift has occurred in our cultural expectation of a primary partnership. We live in the age of the individual. We want to be happy. Women are more independent. All of these factors feed a more serially monogamous pattern of behaviour. Author and marriage historian Stephanie Coontz says that relationships have altered more in the past thirty years than in the 3,000 before. So breakups and more blended versions of family have become part of our landscape. And often that means letting go of the idea that we have to feel threatened by an ex-partner's new partner…or by a partner's ex.

Comedian Lucy Frederick has spoken onstage and in the press about her friendship with Emily, the former wife of her partner James and the mother of his two children. Writing in the *Guardian* last year, she said, 'The term stepmother still has the whiff of an austere lady sending her new partner's children off to boarding school. But I was keen to take on the moniker. I don't want to be "Daddy's girlfriend". I want to be a legitimate part of this family. And family means Emily too.' Guesting on *The Breakup Monologues,* she described a Halloween party that happened while James and Emily were still living together as amicable housemates and co-parents after their conscious uncoupling: 'I was there, her boyfriend was there, they opened a bottle of champagne that had been given to them when they got married...it was all very civilised but lots of people felt that it was weird.' Eventually it was the kids that suggested that maybe Mum and Dad didn't need to live together any more.

One of the particularly poignant aspects of a breakup is when, without a reason like children for everyone to keep in touch, you no longer see your ex-partner's family. Some of the happiest days I spent with Nice Ex-Girlfriend were when we popped up to Potter's Bar to spend time with her mum and grandmother. Her grandmother's house was very elegant and tidy. Yet Nice Ex-Girlfriend's mum had an adorably cheeky dog called Roxy who would often break antique ornaments, lick the cream off the top of the trifle, or surreptitiously and silently climb the bookcase in order to reach a bowl of gently salted cashew nuts which had been carefully placed out of the way while we were chatting and having lunch. Fortunately her grandmother was a very calm woman who would always brush off these mishaps with a carefree, 'Oh...it doesn't matter.' And we would all laugh.

Perhaps it was then that I first realised how animals, like children, can bond us adult humans together.

23

Healthy Space...and a bit about Attachment Theory

1 year 9 months A.G. (After Girlfriend)

'We've got to get off this train now and get onto another one. Are you ready?'

Dog tilts her head and stares at me quizzically. Normally I can't bring myself to be authoritative with this tiny creature with oversized eyes, ears and paws. So I just say things like 'Oh sweetie you're not supposed to do that' in a cutesy voice and then think, 'Oh shit, I was supposed to tell her off.' But Girlfriend, who normally plays 'bad cop' if required, is away for a few days at a conference.

In her absence, I have delighted in emptying the dishwasher top rack first. She thinks that this is foolish, as the items drip onto the bottom rack. But I don't care. Free from her domestic scrutiny, I can leave two pieces of toilet paper on the roll without changing it. She hates this. Her preferred etiquette is for the roll to be changed if it's that close to the end. But what am I supposed to do with the superfluous two sheets? That would suffice for my next wee, surely?

Who needs to have an affair when there are so many tiny ways to be subversive?

Girlfriend's absence also means that I am Dog's default alpha. Suddenly I'm the one she looks to for instruction. So how better to really test this temporarily elevated status than to take Dog on a complicated tube journey involving lots of changes at rush hour on a sweltering Friday night?

I'm enjoying the additional presence I have in the world. Everyone looks and smiles when you have a cute animal by your side. As a double act, Dog and I are crushing it.

We are headed to my gig, a double-bill preview show with The Bisexual Comedian. The word 'preview' normally implies that one is headed to Edinburgh Fringe. But of course I have broken up with Edinburgh. So instead I'm previewing a show for literary, arts and science festivals, ones that pay artists and treat them properly.

The Moon & Maybe cafe in Ealing is just the kind of bohemian haven that I thrive in. A tiny stage next to the entrance allows for amiable mockery of latecomers as they apologetically tiptoe along the extensive counter full of enticing cakes to find a seat. The back of the venue opens into a cosy backyard of palm trees, potted plants, sofas and fairy lights.

Angie arrives and coos over Dog. She's had one of her famously dramatic public breakups with Liz, the sort that prompts strangers to intervene and check on their welfare.

I really feel for her. I know how it aches to be locked by your own insecurity and pain into a relationship so fragile and combustible that any moment could be the trigger, the thing that breaks you up. The gun would've been loaded all along. But one tiny moment could send the fatal bullet hurtling down the barrel.

To leave permanently is unthinkable. The danger and drama is an addiction. And when you leave an addiction behind, you are empty. The thing that has filled you up is gone. Yet amidst all the attrition, a respite is essential now and then. Hence the yoyo pattern of constant breakups and reunions.

Although Angie looks tired and stressed as she enthusiastically slurps at a large glass of red, she seems bigger, brighter and better. She is 'fun Angie'. Perhaps it's an elaborate act of escapism. But there's a certain freedom about her when she is temporarily disengaged from her heart-wrenching battle with impossible love.

We both know how inevitable it is that Liz will come back, and that Angie will take her back thinking, 'This time…*this* time around, it's going to be OK.' But it never really is. A study published in the *Journal of Family Relations* discovered links between 'relationship cycling' and depression and anxiety. Each round of the on-and-off cycle tends to degrade the quality of the relationship, a bit like a jpeg image deteriorating each time it's opened, edited and saved again. Every new iteration is a little worse, leaving the couple stranded together in a limbo somewhere between fully together and fully apart. Even in relationships so abusive that a woman has to call a family violence helpline for professional advice, the average number of times she returns to her partner before leaving for good is seven. As advice columnist Beth McColl says, 'Sometimes love is not a phoenix. It's just a horrible goose that steals your bread, bites your hand and runs off into the lake.'[1]

In terms of the psychology of what is known as 'attachment theory',[2] Liz and Angie bear all the hallmarks of a classic anxious-avoidant pairing. They're actually pretty common pairings, even though they can be horribly painful to be in. Whenever avoidant Liz is reticent to commit and asks for some space, it triggers anxious Angie to demand even more closeness. Although the basic premise of this theory is that each of us has a relatively consistent attachment style throughout our lifetime, there

---

1   However, intriguingly, couples that have just one break seem to thrive quite well. Tennis champion Andy Murray and his wife Kim Sears met at a US Open party in 2005 when he was eighteen. Kim was then a permanent fixture in Andy's support team at tournaments for the next few years…until they split for a few months in 2009. They confirmed their reunion in 2010. Andy went on to win three Grand Slams, bag two Olympic Golds and marry Kim in 2015, keeping his wedding ring safe at subsequent matches by tying it to his shoelaces. Awww. Similarly Prince William's route to romantic happiness with Kate Middleton took a slight detour in 2007 when they also split for a few months. They were both photographed going out separately and having fun, wild times as singletons. According to one royal biographer, Kate only accepted William back into her life on the condition that he had no further contact with a former love interest. Some surveys suggest that 50 per cent of couples that break up get back together again. Perhaps it's a case of realising that you had it pretty good after all when you see what other horrors are out there! I wonder if Andy or Wills tried Tinder?!

2   Attachment theory was originally formulated by psychiatrist John Bowlby. His primary area of interest was in infants and their relationships to adult caregivers. In the 1980s, the theory was extended to attachment in adults. A *very* basic summary is that we are all somewhere on an 'anxious' scale and somewhere on an 'avoidant' scale. If you have low scores for both of these, you are 'secure'. Studies suggest that about 58 per cent of people are secure. That means one hell of a lot of people are insecure in some way, whether that's anxious, avoidant or oscillating between the two in an unresolved attachment style. Breakups tend to hurt anxiously attached adults the most, due to their greater fear of abandonment. This fear typically stems from childhood experience.

is evidence that we can adapt if we choose a more secure partner, as I have with Girlfriend. We did a free online test recently and each came out as 'secure' with low scores for both anxiety and avoidance, but both admitted we would have answered the questions very differently when we were in our previous relationships. And I might well answer them differently if I was being quizzed about my platonic friendships, a place where I habitually feel on less steady ground.

Yet, right now in this moment, in this temporary ceasefire between Angie and Liz, it feels like I have my friend back from the warzone that typically occupies her. And I rather like it.

We are engaged in some daft giggly banter about how pervy cats like to watch their owners have sex when The Bisexual Comedian arrives. It must be nearly time for me to go onstage. I start to give Angie instructions for looking after Dog during my set.

'Here's her blanket to put down under the table. She'll lie on that. But you could give her a chew if she won't settle.'

'Blimey, it's like a woman handing her baby over. I do know dogs. She'll be fine, Wilby.'

'Sorry, yes, of course. I'm fussing like a total idiot.'

After my show and selling and signing a few books in the interval, I join Angie to watch The Bisexual Comedian's performance. My default mode is to run off home after gigs, after my work is done. Yet here, in such a friendly setting, everyone paying attention to Dog, with a glass of good wine, a good friend and my fantasy new best friend entertaining us, I am in my element. I could stay here forever. As if to acknowledge this need to freeze time, my watch stops.

As The Bisexual Comedian commands the stage with a serene unapologetic confidence, the straight, white, middle-class audience all nodding in recognition, a realisation hits me. Suddenly I understand how our tiny interaction came to have such a disproportionately seismic impact on me. She broke my heart, not so much because she rejected me but because her relative position of privilege in the world opened my eyes to how many doors have always been closed to me. Until I met her, I had been standing so far away from those doors of opportunity that I couldn't even see them in the first place. Whether she is aware of it or not, her experience is coloured by living well within mainstream norms. Whatever her inner desires, her outward-facing identity is more accepted than mine.

Perhaps this says something about the limitations of labels more than it does about her. If we could just describe our sexual orientations as colours and say, 'I feel a bit orange…or green…or purple today,' then that might better demonstrate the difference between our chameleonic lusts and the political and cultural identities that have historically been attached, in both celebratory and derogatory ways, to ideas of queerness or otherness. For me, being gay has been about so much more than fancying women. It made me an outsider. That was both limiting and liberating. So long as we are alert to the dangers of creating fragments and hierarchies within our own community, perhaps it is progress if slowly but surely we all start to become insiders and continue to create change from there.

And, with all that in mind, I have to confess that I really benefit from being in the same room as The Bisexual Comedian. For all the contradictions and questions that she brings up for me, she's a warm, generous person who bothers to say, 'You were really good' after I come offstage. Whether we ever develop the close friendship I once dreamed of or remain friendly colleagues who simply have a good laugh whenever we work together, I feel at peace with our past.

As Angie and I head towards the tube, with Dog obediently trotting next to us, The Bisexual Comedian calls after us, 'Anyone want a lift anywhere?' I toy fleetingly with that old daydream of heading off at last on our *Thelma & Louise* road trip. 'No, we're fine thanks. The tube's only a few minutes down the road.' After all, fantasy people are always unreliable and fucked-up in real life.

When Dog and I finally collapse through the door, I sit down in the hallway wiping her paws with an old towel. It's not really necessary tonight but has become a habit. She lifts each leg up in turn, knowing the routine. I gaze into her hazel eyes and lean in to kiss the top of her head, inhaling her warm biscuity smell as her tail beats a happy rhythm against the wall.

Although I'm looking forward to Girlfriend getting home, being apart for a couple of days has been so valuable. It opened up a space for me to find connection, a space that seems healthier and more balanced than the fraught gap between Angie and Liz.

And perhaps that space enabled me to let go of some old ghosts.

24

The Good Breakup

2 years A.G. (After Girlfriend)

'I have a message for Rosie. Her book *Is Monogamy Dead?* is not only brilliant but also features a cameo role from me, for reasons that didn't feel kind to Rosie at the time. Hearing her now, and having seen her several times since, I'm struck by how lucky her partner is and how lucky I was to encounter her back then. I'm sorry if I caused any hurt. Peace out, lovely Rosie! PS Rosie knows who I am. I'll leave it to her as to whether she'd like to keep this anonymous or not.'

Peering over presenter Suzy Klein's shoulder in the Radio 4 *Saturday Live* studio, I feel a huge dopamine hit of validation. The Bisexual Comedian is not only listening to me discussing my podcasting 'success' story on air, she has bothered to send in a message. It lights up the computer screen and is the only one of a stream of comments, the majority intended for the more famous guests, that I can see.

It seems an odd thing for her to do. If she really had felt a sudden need to apologise for her rejection of me all that time ago, she could just message me directly. Even so, her acknowledgement of my value in the world means something. I have proved that I'm not someone to be dismissed so easily. I feel like Leonardo DiCaprio's character Cobb in the film *Inception*. I am slowly changing her perception of what happened, planting an idea, fixing something over years and years in a deep sub-level of a dream. Maybe one day I will wake up and still be young.

I have harnessed this funny little breakup, this fleeting unrequited crush that disproportionately troubled me, and I have reclaimed it. A painful experience is transformed into a galvanising, motivating one. I have thrived and grown in its aftermath, getting sponsorship for a radio show, launching a podcast, getting a new agent and book deal, and getting better gigs and opportunities. Perhaps that's why I held onto this breakup even when it didn't seem to warrant such scrutiny...because I could see its potential.[1]

After the initial chaos has dissipated, breakups can have very good side-effects. A 2003 study published in the academic journal *Personal Relationships* and co-authored by writer and speaker Ty Tashiro and Patricia Frazier found that a group of ninety-two undergraduates who had experienced a recent romantic breakup reported, on average, five positive types of personal growth they thought might improve their future romantic relationships. These ranged from boosted self-confidence to learning how to be a better partner and, perhaps most crucially of all, how to choose a better partner. Women reported more growth than men did.[2]

In a recent *Diva* magazine interview, star of the film *Portrait of a Lady on Fire* Adèle Haenel said, 'Maybe it's not a failure when a love story ends. Maybe it lives within you and changes you forever.' Meanwhile *How to be Hopeful* author and podcaster Bernadette Russell says, 'Breakups can bring with them the discomfort of uncertainty but also the exciting possibility that something wonderful could be on its way.' And Stanford University post-doctoral fellow Lauren Howe, who has studied relationship endings, says, 'By seeing breakups as opportunities, people can harness them for self-improvement'. This transformative power of a breakup is often very apparent in the way that somebody embraces life afterwards.

---

1 And because I'm not planning to sabotage my life by breaking up with Girlfriend, a really great real-life partner, this is the most recent motivational discomfort I can find. Lucky me, I guess.

2 Although I do wonder if there are, loosely speaking, two types of women – those who feel supported by relationships and those who feel suppressed by them. When I guested on *The High Low Show* podcast, the two hosts were an example of this binary. Pandora Sykes openly admitted to feeling lifted up by a partner, whereas Dolly Alderton, like me, indicated that she thrives more when she is single. It makes me wonder why women in this latter category pursue romantic relationships at all. It seems counterintuitive. It's almost as if we are actively pursuing a breakup. Comedian Juliet Meyers, happily single, likens the awkward restrictiveness of coupledom to doing pair exercises at a workshop: 'I'll be fairly easygoing, they'll think they know better than me, I'll be polite but pissed off...and then I will think... "I'm so happy alone."'

After she got dumped from a nine-year partnership, one of my Facebook friends started a 'breakup list' of daily new challenges, all the sporting activities she'd wanted to have a go at, and places she'd wanted to visit but had become diverted from by the cosiness of commitment. Journalist Kate Spicer says, 'Breakups can be very cleansing, like a psychedelic experience. With hindsight, they're magical...an idyll, where you can get yourself back.' Mia Levitin launched her dream career as a cultural critic in the wake of her divorce, finding that being single motivated her to dig deeper for her inner resilience. Writing in *Red* magazine, she says, 'Sometimes we're better off not getting what we think we want.'

Comedian and podcaster Sam Baines describes having an explosive post-separation reclamation of her sexuality, feeling 'astounded and thrilled that people fancied me after so long out of the game'. It coincided with the 'empowering and uplifting' experience of performing in the West End show *Magic Mike* and 'speaking to 300 women every night about loving your body'. And famously, Sarah Millican embarked upon a stellar comedy career after her divorce, discussing in interviews how she needed to 'hit the bottom in order to bounce back up again'.

Meanwhile, John Robins and Sara Pascoe both wrote about their 2016 Christmas breakup in their 2017 Edinburgh Fringe shows. He went on to win the Edinburgh Comedy Award for *The Darkness of Robins*, in which he pedantically found comfort in the tiny victories of newly single life (a 25 per cent single person's council tax discount and knowing where the iPhone charger cable is), and she had five-star reviews and acclaim for her show *LadsLadsLads*, in part inspired by an awful breakup recovery yoga retreat in Costa Rica.

It's almost as if these people have all harnessed the intensity of their emotion, the very same primal hurt that can push us towards destructive acts of revenge,[3] and repurposed it as a force for good. This is the opposite narrative to the one we so often hear – that staying together is 'good' and breaking up is 'bad'. Around the world, across cultures, a separation is seen as a shameful thing. So much so that photographs of a woman carrying a 'Divorced and Happy' sign at an International

---

3 One of the exhibits at Zagreb's Museum of Broken Relationships is the axe that a Berlin woman used to chop up her former lover's furniture. These acts of revenge may seem incredibly therapeutic at the time. But if we can use that same energy to start a new project, it may serve us better in the long run.

Women's Day march in Pakistan caused a global ruckus on Twitter. But what if that narrative is wrong? What if a breakup is a vital piece of the grand puzzle of discovering our sense of self?

When something has hurt us we feel rearranged, as if our limbs and vital organs are in different places. This rebuilding can sometimes be a truly wonderful thing. I describe this type of liberated happy-sad rebirth as 'breakup energy', an idea that Dolly Alderton sums up really well: 'When you've been dumped, it engenders this odd freedom. You make yourself your own project because suddenly you only have yourself to worry about. You're creating a fun new story for yourself. That kind of fury, outrage, sadness and humiliation can be converted into something.'

Journalist and author Helen Croydon thinks that we often seek out something in a newly single life that is the opposite of the thing we didn't quite like in a relationship. When her partnership with a pub-loving 'bon viveur' ended, she was propelled into doing something a bit more 'worthwhile' with her weekends than extended boozy lunches. She joined her local running club, the Victoria Park Harriers. It was a dramatic lifestyle change for a former party girl who admits that she had once 'loathed the outdoors'. She entered the London Triathlon and kept up a gruelling training regime through the rain and hail, eventually qualifying for the World Championships.

Poet Kate Fox has found herself unexpectedly falling in love again in the aftermath of the end of her ten-year marriage. She describes the space she now occupies as 'liminal', where everything is 'up for grabs'. This flux is something she believes that she may be a bit addicted to. After all, being in a threshold state between two worlds suggests that we are on the verge of something new. And that can be incredibly thrilling: 'My marriage was long, stable and together and that was probably me moving away from being liminal. That's a long time not to be liminal. And now I'm back, I'm thinking, "Oh I missed this up in the air place."'

The notion of separating from her husband first germinated when she started swimming outdoors[4]: 'Seven years ago, I began regular trips to Helmsley Pool…which was around the same time that we got the dog and stopped having sex.[5] Each year I found myself counting down

---

4 Because Kate is proudly Northern, she doesn't like the pretentious whiff of the phrase 'wild swimming'.
5 Because they started calling each other 'Mummy' and 'Daddy' and had their primary focus shifted away from each other, much as parents of human babies do.

the days until the pool opened. It became more and more important. Swimming was me keeping in touch with me and how I flow in the world. I realised I needed to not have to wait until the summer and went on solo expeditions to discover lakes, rivers and go in the sea. It was during August when I was doing a lot of swimming in Scotland that I somehow just knew that if I was alright while I was swimming, I would be alright on my own.'

The UK parliamentary delays to the introduction of a 'no-fault' divorce bill mean that couples like Kate and her ex still have to cite reasons for separating, under the old-school categories such as 'adultery' or 'unreasonable behaviour', even though they remain amicable. Kate says wistfully, 'It turns out that "I have discovered myself through swimming outside" and "we got a dog and couldn't have sex any more" are apparently not legitimate reasons that you can put down.'[6]

When I hear about breakups like this, where the underlying friendship and mutual respect has been so carefully preserved, I wonder if we need to revise our thinking about monogamy. If only we could swim out on our own towards liminality and the new adventures just beyond it, whilst also maintaining the deep companionship that is entwined with having a long history with someone. Non-monogamy isn't for everyone. But, even if we stick to monogamy, perhaps we can look to our polyamorous friends for inspiration as to how to think about breakups differently.

6   Just as I'm finishing up this book, Kate posts on Facebook about how efficient, quick and easy the online divorce service is. A new law was introduced in the UK in April 2019 which meant that couples would no longer have to blame each other for the breakdown of a marriage. But it was held up passing through parliament because of Brexit.

25

Poly Breakups

2 years 3 months A.G. (After Girlfriend)

'Thanks Jason. You're doing a great job.'

'Yeah I should get finished tomorrow. Anyway, I've got to get back to my wife and girlfriend now.'

We glance at one another as if to check in and telepathically say, 'Does he mean two different people?'

He does.

Jason, a stubbly handsome-in-the-right-light friend of a friend is laying some new garden decking for us. We have barely chatted to him all day. But now our intrigued glance seems to have opened up the floodgates for him to tell us all about his amazing life with his two women.

I am genuinely very interested in the concept of non-monogamy, from a theoretical standpoint at least. In my view, the emotional honesty and grownup communication I have witnessed in people who do ethical multiple relationships[1] well are something we should all aspire to in our monogamous relationships.

Yet this guy is an exhibitionist bore. He dropped it into conversation because he really wants to show off. I thought he might like to hear about the comedy show and book I wrote exploring this whole world. But no, he does not.

Eventually, he swaggers out to his van and is gone.

'Bloody hell, he goes on a bit, doesn't he?'

---

1   A US study published in *The Journal of Sex and Marital Therapy* in 2018 suggested that more than one in five adults has been in a consensual non-monogamous relationship.

'I thought you were interested.'

'I'm interested in the concept, not in his bravado.'

'I think he's bringing his girlfriend tomorrow.'

'That'll be fun. If she's hot, shall we have an orgy?'

Girlfriend knows I'm joking. But just to make absolutely certain that I know that this is off the table, she issues a flat, 'No'.

It turns out that the girlfriend is almost cliché levels of hot, in Lara Croft shorts with drills and hammers dangling from her tool belt and a floppy dark fringe constantly falling in front of her face.

'Blimey. He's done well. No wonder his ego is a bit out of control.'

But even if a parade of a hundred hot women was going on in our garden right now, we wouldn't particularly care. We are exclusive and happily so.

Yet I haven't always had such an easy relationship with monogamy...

When I was with Nice Ex-Girlfriend, it seemed senseless to throw all the good, stable things about our partnership away over something as trivial as sex. However, neither of us really wanted to give up on sex forever either. For about a year towards the end, we lived in an ambiguous limbo and had hypothetical conversations about what the ground rules would be if either of us wanted to bring someone back to the house. But I felt incredibly lonely as I noncommittally ventured out more and more to meet new friends and potential new secondary love interests. I realised I did not want a casual lover, or even casual friends for that matter. I wanted depth. And perhaps I wanted that with just one person after all.

Yet it is in my desire to maintain a closeness with Nice Ex-Girlfriend that I see some crossover with a polyamorous mindset.

Since comedian and activist Kate Smurthwaite became polyamorous she reckons splitting up has been far easier: 'In monogamy world, breakups have to be final. You have to draw a clear line to free yourself to start something new. I don't do that. When James, my primary, and I split up we kept hold of so many of the good bits. We work together, we sometimes have dinner, he comes round for Christmas, we cuddle...we even have the odd snog. No new monogamous partner would tolerate such a close relationship with an ex.'

She's right. Girlfriend would not be keen at all on Nice Ex-Girlfriend and I having an occasional snog. And, to be brutally honest, I don't think either I or Nice Ex-Girlfriend would have any desire to go back there. We have moved forwards into a new kind of friendship. But there is a certain kind of intimacy that is wrapped up with having shared several years of your life with someone, even if it's just common memories and tedious in-jokes.[2] Although it is a purely platonic connection and has none of the intensity of a romantic relationship, it still has a different texture to 'just friends'.

Evolutionary psychologists Diana Fleischman and Geoffrey Miller are primary partners who guested on season two of *The Breakup Monologues*. He says, 'It's a big hidden cost to monogamy that you learn about somebody and create a bond, then if something goes wrong and they're not quite your ideal partner, you're supposed to just jettison them and treat them as if they never meant anything. With poly, you don't have to make that pretence. You don't have to break up with somebody just because they're not a perfect fit in every way. You're not doing this high-wire act where you're saying, "We could be together forever"…or…"I'm just going to eject you forever from my life."'

However, Diana adds that some people have the opposite problem – they never break up with anyone and become 'poly hoarders' with, say, fifteen casual partners. 'You do have to clear the decks every so often,' she laughs.

This ethical couple are so respectful to the primary partnership that they even try and ensure that any separations with secondary lovers happen while the other one is away, and preferably uncontactable. They want to avoid bringing in negative energy from the breakup back into their partnership. Diana says, 'I broke up with someone while Geoffrey was at Burning Man. So that there was no way I would lean on him about it.'

Kathy Labriola is author of *The Polyamory Breakup Book*. She says, 'It is very challenging to be fully present physically and emotionally in your remaining relationships when you are so devastated by a breakup with a lover. When you go through a monogamous breakup, you can wallow in self-pity, endlessly processing with your ex about whose fault everything was, spending hours contemplating revenge, hiding in your

---

2   Tedious for everyone else, that is.

room crying and cyberstalking your ex and their new lovers on social media, and drinking yourself to sleep every night. Whereas when you go through a poly breakup, you probably still have at least one other serious relationship that you are hoping will still be there when you get over the worst of this navel-gazing.' She advises communicating that you are not at your best but will try to still be available and present for quality time with them.

It was only really when I started meeting poly friends that I understood that a relationship can still be thought of as a success even if it ends. Perhaps it can continue in a new form or perhaps not. Either way, maybe it was fun and enriching for the time that it worked well, like a seasonal flower that bloomed and then withered away organically. The initial expectation wouldn't necessarily have been the kind of monogamous anticipation we have for a lifelong all-or-nothing soulmate connection. Polyamory factors in celebrations of other intimacies outside of the sexual and, as such, allows for different types of endings. Many poly couples even stay living together and raising children together after a breakup, often moving their new lovers into the house as well.

Between the late 1960s and 1980s, there were several poly communal families in San Francisco known as Keristans. They practised a form of group marriage known as 'polyfidelity', where everyone was exclusive within the group. When marriages ended they made gradual transitions from romantic to platonic connections known as 'graceful distancing', in a precursor to modern terminologies like conscious uncoupling and respectful space. The theory was that a less abrupt, dramatic or one-sided breakup gives both people a chance to start spending time with other lovers and friends, gradually rebuilding their support system. A few years ago, I mooted the idea of a 'decompression year' on social media to describe a similar mutually agreed transitioning.

In a foreword to Kathy's book, author of famed tome *The Ethical Slut* Dossie Easton says, 'Many of our relationships work best if they're allowed to run their natural course. For some, they can be considered as serving a purpose, and then when we have learned what we needed to, it's time to accept an end. Such connections might last weeks, months or years, but duration is not the measure of their value.'

My takeaway from all this is that I'm not great at non-monogamy but there are a ton of great principles attached to it which could make breakups less traumatic.

Yet in the near future, whether we are monogamous or polyamorous, traumatic breakups might become a thing of the past. We might be able to take something called an 'anti-love drug' to help us get over an ex.

26

My Chemical Romance?

2 years 5 months A.G. (After Girlfriend)

'I get emails from people saying, "I'm in a relationship that I can rationally see is no good for me. Yet the thought of leaving it is emotionally excruciating. If only I could take some drug to allow me to achieve my higher order goal of severing what feels like an addiction." In the future, oxytocin blockers may well be able to serve that role.'

I am interviewing Brian D. Earp. He is a co-author of the book *Love is the Drug* and an associate director of the Ethics and Health Policy programme at the New York bioethics research institute and think tank, The Hastings Centre. I've been aware of his ideas around 'anti-love drugs' for some time. In the near future, he believes that we might be able to chemically manipulate our emotions in order to reduce the traumatic effects of a breakup.[1]

As he pours tea from a gigantic pot in his friend's Stoke Newington living room, he tells me about the so-called 'cuddle chemical', the bonding hormone oxytocin, and about some experiments that have been carried out on prairie voles, a species often used in studies of pair bonding. They form particularly strong, exclusive connections with a mate due to a sophisticated system of dense oxytocin receptors. Yet when female prairie voles are injected with an oxytocin blocker, they lose their

---

1   Brian is also researching 'love drugs', such as MDMA, that could help us through a rocky patch in a relationship and help us to avoid a breakup. MDMA was widely used during the 1980s in a therapeutic context in couples counselling and psychotherapy before it was outlawed as a rave drug.

monogamous tendencies and no longer exhibit a partner preference. If that female prairie vole was trying to liberate herself from an abusive relationship with a particularly controlling male prairie vole who had a powerful emotional hold over her, that might be a very good thing.

Although many scientists believe that humans possess some very similar bonding mechanisms, we haven't yet been tested in the lab in quite the same way.

But there is evidence that some drugs that many of us already take might dampen our romantic and sexual bonds in a similarly dramatic fashion. SSRIs, or selective serotonin reuptake inhibitors, are a group of antidepressants which, alongside their main task of combating depression, have all kinds of interpersonal side effects that we haven't yet measured properly.

'We tend to label drugs in terms of their intended purpose,' says Brian, 'but the drugs don't know that they're an antidepressant. That's one of the effects that they have for some people. One reasonably well-measured side effect of SSRIs is that they can dampen libido. And in a subset of people, SSRIs have the effect of making it harder for you to care about the feelings of others. So, if there's somebody that you're attached to and you want to create some emotional distance, the side effects of these drugs could, in a clumsy way, partially achieve that.'

And there you have it. An anti-love drug.

He cites case studies of people who went onto antidepressants and reported falling 'out of love' with their partner. In these cases, it was an unwanted effect.

Yet if a person is in an abusive relationship they want to leave, perhaps this might be a desirable effect, one that they might want to seek out. Perhaps these undocumented side effects could be harnessed in order to help us escape bad relationships.

Obsessive compulsive disorder is often treated with an SSRI. Perhaps obsessive unhealthy love isn't so very different.[2]

The idea of an 'anti-love drug' reminds me a little of the memory erasure process depicted in one of my all-time favourite films, *Eternal Sunshine of the Spotless Mind*. I had always assumed it was pure science

---

2 Sometimes I think the histrionics of the relationship between Angie and Liz look a lot like a kind of depression or mental illness. So perhaps it makes sense that, if either or both ever wanted to leave, the 'treatment' would be an antidepressant that would promote a sense of calm.

fiction. The plot centres on shy Joel and free spirit Clementine who meet on a train in Montauk without realising that they are former lovers who both visited a curious company called Lacuna Inc to wipe their memories of the relationship. Even when they both discover what has happened, they decide that their connection is strong enough to give it another chance.

Yet it seems this science fiction could be closer to science fact than I realised. Brian tells me about a Canadian psychiatrist and post-traumatic stress disorder expert, Alain Brunet, who performs what he calls 'reconsolidation therapy': 'People dealing with romantic trauma come into the lab and Alain asks them to recall specific memories associated with that partner while taking a beta blocker called propranolol. The drug suppresses some of the emotional response they might have to those memories. So when the person experiences them without feeling gripped by despair, they re-record them. If they do this enough times, the content of the memory remains but the emotional sting will have been deadened by the procedure.'

So rather than Joel's memories completely disintegrating around him as the walls collapse and the sea floods his bedroom, he could simply have removed the traumatic aspect of thinking about Clementine. Although that might not have made quite such an exquisite film.

However, when I meet psychologist Kimberley Wilson at a podcasting event, she expresses some concern: 'The post-traumatic growth after having your heart broken is important. Everything contributes to the experience of who you are.' So if we do ever get to a point where we can simply delete negative memories, we might avoid identifying unhealthy patterns and we could end up repeating cycles of bad relationships. There's an idea that 'what isn't processed is repeated'. Perhaps that is why Joel and Clementine get back together at the end of the film. After all, Madrid-born philosopher George Santayana once said, 'Those who cannot remember the past are condemned to repeat it.'

Brian says, 'One of the main concerns people have about memory-altering interventions is that there isn't a universal line we can draw in the sands of human suffering. Perhaps it will be down to the judgements of the individual. Maybe it's a durational thing. You might say, "It's been a year since my breakup and I can barely get out of bed. I certainly haven't been able to think about dating other people." If you're in that much despair, there are major opportunity costs there. You're not able to engage with other things of value in your life. On the other hand, if you've gone through a breakup and it kind of hurts but, instead of dealing with any of the trauma, you want to find a quick route out of something that you really ought to be learning from…then you can see that could be a mistake.'

As I'm listening to Brian talking so passionately about his work, it strikes me that I have unwittingly undergone my own version of 'reconsolidation therapy'.

On the evening of my breakup with Secretive Ex-Girlfriend, I had a preview gig booked at Southwark Playhouse. I was in such a tearful, shaky state that I decided to phone the promoter, a cute guy called Simon who I always described as 'a bit like Jude Law's geeky brother', to investigate cancellation options.

'Simon, I'm not sure I can do the gig tonight. My girlfriend broke up with me. I'm a mess. And my show is all about love and our relationship. It feels meaningless now. I'll feel like an idiot doing that material.'

'Oh no…I'm really sorry Rosie. It's totally up to you. But I think you can do this. You can chat to the audience and be honest about what's happened. They'll be on your side. They're a lovely bunch of regulars who have all bought tickets specifically to see you.'

'How many tickets have we sold?'

'I think it's a sellout. About a hundred or so.'

'Crikey. Scary!'

'Don't be scared. They know it's a preview show. So you could have notes if you need to.'

'I suppose I *could* just be really honest right at the top of the show…'

'Yeah.'

'And it's probably better than sitting here on my own.'

'I'm sure it will be. I'll be really looking forward to seeing you and the show.'

'Can I think for five minutes and call you right back Simon?'

'Of course.'

I did the show, my own version of what I call 'a Tig Notaro'. Tig is a brilliant American comedian whose second live album is a raw, emotional recording of a set that she performed at her regular monthly show at Largo in Los Angeles just four days after being diagnosed with breast cancer. Although I can only dream of creating something quite as magical as she did, I experienced something of a similar effect. I was completely authentic and sad onstage, talking honestly and veering off script. My normal silly routines about the petty annoyances of staying in a relationship felt redundant. A new show, all about the breakup, was born. Sharing my shock and grief with a hundred empathetic strangers made me feel lighter. Maybe my partner did not love me any more. But, for fifty minutes, these people did. I couldn't stop smiling on the bus home, my phone alight with messages from friends who had been in the audience.

And then I told the story again and again. Instead of a beta blocker, my drug had been the audience's laughter. I had reduced the trauma attached to these memories by making them funny, by sharing them.

A few years later, I didn't need to tell the story any more. There were other stories to tell.

27

Towards a Growth Mindset

2 years 5 months A.G. (After Girlfriend)

'Would you ever take an anti-love drug?'

'I'm too square. And anyway, we learn from our experiences. Everything happens for a reason. We may not know what that reason is. But it's there to serve us in some way and I wouldn't want to miss out on that.'

Blimey, I suddenly feel like I'm going out with the Dalai Lama. Perhaps I had been too quick to judge Girlfriend in the past as a shallow fun seeker, just because she likes to throw parties and socialise. She might be the more spiritual, conscious one after all.[1]

We are, however, on our way to a party. The *Diva* Awards are just about to get underway at the Waldorf Hilton in the West End. We are walking from the train station in our dresses searching for somewhere to change out of our old trainers into heels. We settle on the lobby of the slightly less posh hotel next door and bundle the trainers into a plastic bag, ready to deposit swiftly in the cloakroom. We always feel like fish out of water at these black tie events. Yet we are grateful to be invited,

---

1   There's a certain irony to the fact that I've spent three years interviewing people about breakups and how they shape our lives. And it's possible that the person I should've been asking was right in front of me all along.

even when we are clearly a last-minute addition to the guest list after someone higher profile has pulled out.

Hobbling awkwardly in the unfamiliar shoes, we search for our place cards. 'Here we are,' I say with a wave to Girlfriend from a table in the corner, farthest away from the stage.

I've got to present one of the first awards, to Hannah Bardell for Politician of the Year. This will apparently happen between the starter and the main course. I'd better not get too distracted by food and not leave myself enough time to totter all the way across the room on the hellish high heels. I consider timing a practice run while everyone is still milling around.

Paralympian and chief executive of the brilliant charity Diversity Role Models, Claire Harvey, and her partner Helen join us at our table. Claire is in a wheelchair. So Girlfriend thoughtfully slides the chair out to make space for her. Helen slides it back in. Girlfriend, already slightly pissed on a few sips of the free wine and still really, really keen to be helpful, slides it out again. Helen puts the chair back in and Claire lifts herself out of her wheelchair into the chair at the table. Girlfriend puts her head in her hands and says, 'I'm so sorry. I've had a horror there.' Claire and Helen generously laugh it off.

It's all fine but yet again we feel like dickheads who do the wrong thing and don't quite belong. 'I've just danced a really un-PC hokey-cokey with Claire Harvey *MBE*,' she whispers, as if the three letters printed after her name on the place card make it all the more mortifying. 'I think it'll be OK,' I whisper back.

Before the night is out, Girlfriend has become best mates with Claire Harvey and knows everything there is to know about seated volleyball. I manage to articulately present an award without any mishaps and then discreetly slip off the uncomfortable shoes under the table.

But there is a slight melancholy puncturing my fun evening. I'm in the middle of yet another professional breakup. It's more on my own terms than my breakup with my agent was. I think I might be learning how to control the situation better and avoid allowing myself to melt into such an emotional mess. Perhaps I'm becoming more acclimatised to loss, more accepting of it. Maybe greater exposure to it increases your immunity, a bit like a vaccine. Yet however familiar this situation is, and however much I have pulled through and survived it before, I still don't like how it feels.

I'm at an impasse over money[2] with the producers of the first season of the podcast. Now that the Arts Council funding has run out, I need to find a way of making the show financially self-sufficient in order to carry on doing it. I plan to move the recordings from an intimate studio, which I can no longer afford to hire, to a live setting at London's podcasting hub Kings Place. I'm excited about this new format. But they won't budge on their production price per episode even though it no longer includes studio hire. And even though a total sellout wouldn't provide enough door split income to cover that price. I feel stuck. I've got no real option but to look for another producer who's more flexible and in tune with my grassrootsy indie way of financing things.

On the train home, back in our comfy trainers, I browse my phone and happen to see a post on the Facebook Podcasters Support Group from Dave Pickering, someone I've known for years through a variety of creative projects, including a brilliant live event I often guested at, Stand Up Tragedy. I had forgotten that Dave was involved with podcasting. I start typing a message tentatively sounding out interest in becoming a producer of *The Breakup Monologues*.

I think about what Girlfriend said at the start of the night. Everything happens for a reason. There is a reason why Dave has popped up into my consciousness right now.

I press 'send'.

***

'I love you, ginger.'

'What about when I'm not ginger?'

'What do you mean?'

'When I'm grey!'

'Oh, well my eyes might have gone by then. I probably won't be able to see you very well.'

As another birthday looms, we feel old.

When we discovered we had a birthday on the same day, we each thought the other one was joking. It seemed, to us, an impossibility.

'What are the chances?' we asked.

'One in a million!' exclaimed Glenda.

---

2 Referring back to Kathy's list, it seems like all my professional breakups are down to 'incompatibility around money'.

'Well it's actually one in three hundred and sixty-five,' said my dad, taking us incredibly literally.

Although our more woo-woo astrology friends tell us it means we have some kind of cosmic connection, it's actually a bit of a pain in the arse. Who spoils who with a cup of tea in bed? Who makes a special birthday breakfast?

So we have come away to Bruges so that someone else can spoil us instead. Yet the monosyllabic, slightly stern proprietor of our boutique B&B is hardly a pampering sort. It's incredibly hard work to extract useful information from her.

'I hear there are a lot of lovely markets in Bruges?'

'Yes.'

'Do you know where they are?'

'Yes.'

'...Could you show us, perhaps?'

'Yes.'

Breakfast consists of a teeny tiny pot of muesli and yogurt and a modest buffet of breads, cheese and fruit.

The woman approaches with a notebook.

'Do you like egg?'

We wonder if this means we only get one.

'Yes please.'

'Do you like...scrambled...boiled...?'

This list is taking forever. We have seen a man having a fried egg and are waiting for that option. It doesn't come. So we ask for scrambled.

'They must have run out of fried eggs!' I giggle as she walks away.

We spend the day mooching around drinking hot chocolate and eating waffles with strawberries, ticking all the Bruges tourist activities off the list – boat trip, beer tasting, climbing the bell tower. We try to liven up a tour of the underwhelming chocolate museum by asking the wax models of chocolatiers things like, 'Got any Kit-Kats?'

We are so much more at ease with one another than on our early holidays together. I don't feel the need to be as hypervigilant as I did back in Salisbury. It's almost like we have been able to return to the best selves we were in the honeymoon phase. Now we are more secure, we actively want to make an effort again. No public farting to hear here. And even though I'm due on, she isn't. We have fallen slightly out of sync. So we aren't colliding in hormonal grumpiness in the way that we did on the boat trip.

All that said, it's a slightly strange time of year for me as it's also the anniversary of Mum's death just a couple of days before our birthday, the seventh of September. But then my fleeting sadness lifts when I remember that one of her last real happy times was an art trip to Bruges with Dad. I can feel a real connection with her. Girlfriend is always seeing and hearing signals that she believes are messages from her dad, whether it's a robin in the garden or a car stereo flickering into life when nobody had turned it on. I'm less sure I experience or believe in anything like that. Yet if Mum is ever going to send me a message, I think she's sending one now. And it's a good one. Maybe it's an endorsement of my excellent partner choice…at last. Just as I decide to believe it, the sun comes out from behind the clouds.

At dinner, I am struggling, as I often do, to make a choice about what to have to eat. I'm a perfectionist. I hate to fail and make the wrong choice.

'We can just order something else if you don't like what you get. You've always got such a fixed mindset.'

'What do you mean?'

It isn't a term I am familiar with. So Girlfriend explains that, over a decade ago, Stanford psychologist Carol Dweck identified two distinct mindsets that profoundly influence our achievements and happiness. A fixed mindset assumes that our abilities are static and instils an urgency to prove oneself: 'This is all I've got! So you'd better notice, value and appreciate it!' Whereas a growth mindset is based on a belief that the hand we are dealt is just the starting point. Through application, practice and experience, everyone can develop and grow.

As a child, my dad programmed me to believe that I was intellectually bright, a belief consolidated by my school teachers when I sailed through exams. Yet the rewards of these early successes, and my resultant fear of failure, hampered my ability to learn. Over time this became a disadvantage.

As a young adult, I held on so tightly to bad relationships because I could not possibly fail. I had so much to live up to. Perhaps a breakup is all the more painful to someone with a tendency towards a fixed mindset. I arrogantly assumed that I should be the one to inspire Secretive Ex-Girlfriend to come out, Agoraphobic Ex-Girlfriend to conquer her anxieties, and Boozy Ex-Girlfriend to get a handle on her drinking. Because if I didn't then surely it would invalidate all those things that Dad and my teachers had said about how very clever I was. It would invalidate me. It would shatter the foundations of the domino house that my identity was built on. My self-worth would surely not be recoverable.

But somehow it was…because breakups have been the biggest learning experiences I have had. They have been the few times in my life when I've been forced to adopt more of a growth mindset.

As it turns out, when those relationships did fail, I would surprise myself with a hitherto unknown resilience and I would often thrive during my singleton recovery periods. I would find the confidence to make new friends and start new projects.

Although this is a similar philosophy to the 'fail better' concept that I was trying to apply to love, I hadn't heard it framed in this way before.

In the restaurant, still flapping about what to choose for dinner, I say out loud, 'If only I could be more like "single me" when I'm in a relationship.'

I close my eyes and put a finger on the menu in order to select a dish at random.

I feel a whoosh of relief.

28

Recovery and Reprogramming

Breakup Stories: Charmian Hughes

'I saw a psychotherapist for a year and she said, "This is the script you're in. There are lots of love interests out there but you're not seeing them." It was like she lifted this curse off me. I met my husband quite quickly after that.'

Charmian Hughes, now in her sixties, an established popular circuit comedian and happily married with children, found her feet in life after she escaped from a toxic friendship.

Before she became a performer, she worked in advertising and hated her job. In a state of existential despair and wondering what to do with her life, she started clowning classes at City Lit: 'I was twenty-seven at the time and thought of myself as quite square. Then I met all these performance-y people and a glamorous, free-spirited woman befriended me. I felt chosen and I kind of flowered. It was an exclusive friendship, a bit like a love affair. She used to wear leopard-skin trousers and I started wearing leopard-skin trousers. Over the months and years, I gave a lot of time to her when she'd split up with someone and needed support. I enjoyed that role. I was a bit codependent I suppose. But if anything was upsetting me, I was dismissed as if I was giving her a headache. I started to get self-conscious around her.'

One day, the friend said, 'You're really not that fat', which only exacerbated this self-consciousness. Then at her party, she exclaimed,

'Charmian's arrived, everyone! Stop what you're doing. She's so beautiful…inside.'

Charmian felt like 'the Hunchback of Notre-Dame, the ugly friend who was kept around to make her look good.' She started to seek advice from other people and found the confidence to start performing standup. Yet the more competent she became, the more she felt that her friend 'sabotaged' her.

Then she met a new boyfriend at Edinburgh Fringe, who also treated her badly. When she tried to reach out to her friend, she was told to not be 'so dramatic'. So Charmian had to extract herself from the new romantic relationship with no support from the person that she had listened to for so many years. Once she realised how alone and vulnerable she felt, she started seeing a therapist.

The friend had always told her that she needed to go and travel around India to free herself of her repression. So Charmian bought herself a ticket and went to India during the early stages of recovery from her 'terrible mental state' and started to enjoy her own company. In 1991, India was 'on the borderline of a revolution. There were troops on the streets. You could only go to Goa. So I went to Goa, walked into a bar…and she was there.'

'My heart sank because I'd had such a good time on my own terms with everyone being so lovely to me. We ended up having a fight on a beach. I shouted, "Everything you say is unfair and untrue. That isn't friendship. That is manipulation and hostility." I walked away, with her shouting after me and going bonkers. It was like a rite of passage. I had been allowing myself to be treated like that because I hadn't thought I had any worth at all.'

Through talking to a therapist, Charmian was able to start to see her own worth. It was absolutely the right thing to do. I was in therapy for a few months after my breakup with Nice Ex-Girlfriend. Not so much because it had been the most terrible breakup but because, by then, there was such an accumulation of unprocessed breakups to discuss. Boozy Ex-Girlfriend, Agoraphobic Ex-Girlfriend and Secretive Ex-Girlfriend were all there in a sort of psychological traffic jam.[1] It's no accident that

---

1   The only person I didn't talk about at all with my therapist was The Bisexual Comedian. I thought it was a bit too trivial to bring up in something as serious as a therapy session. But when I started writing this book, she kept coming up. It seemed that she had more of an impact on my interior world than I realised.

my next relationship was the honest, articulate, mature one that I'm in now. Interestingly, Girlfriend was also in therapy for a few months when we started seeing one another.

It's incredible really that many of us wait so long to seek counsel about our relationships. Brian Earp says, 'People feel a little bit all at sea in terms of knowing when a relationship is good or bad, whether it's something they ought to try to maintain or try to leave. I think we do need more guidance from wise people. We don't learn about it in school. We don't take a module in healthy relationships.' It's almost as if we are thrown in the water as young adults and just expected to teach ourselves how to swim. Eventually we do need some proper training. Otherwise we are doing a rudimentary doggy paddle forever.

After his divorce, comedian Gordon Southern sought help from two wildly inappropriate therapists, one who turned out to be a former crack addict. Yet, despite their lack of professionalism, he says, 'The process saved my life.' As a *Chortle* review of his show *That Boy Needs Therapy* suggests, 'If even a woefully reckless therapist can be of some help, just imagine what a good one can do.'

Alongside going to therapy, how else can we best take care of ourselves in the wake of a separation?

Mia Levitin did a meditation course and 'a lot of deliberate forgiveness exercises'. She says, 'My ex went from taking up 99 per cent of my brain space to almost zero!' It also helped to 'accept that the year ahead was going to be crappy and that it was enough to put one foot in front of the other. We've lost the ritual of mourning, so people beat themselves up for not bouncing back right away.'

Sometimes we do need to sit with the sadness for a while before we feel ready for a transformative new start. Speaker, researcher and global phenomenon Brené Brown warns of the dangers of 'over-functioning' at times of anxiety and vulnerability. If we throw ourselves instantly into new challenges, whirlwind flings and endless to-do lists, we might not be fully dealing with our emotions. We risk a burnout.

Co-host of the hit podcast *Scummy Mummies*, Helen Thorn, gave herself permission to be overwhelmed for a short time. She describes days in the aftermath of her separation when she was 'in a raincoat in pyjamas having a secret fag in the back of the garden holding my sixth coffee and wondering what happened.' She suggests that you really do need to 'let yourself cry and listen to the sad song'. As a person who is 'naturally quite sunny', she found that anger was an unfamiliar emotion for her to allow in. Yet there are now more and more days when she can embrace a sense of new opportunity and possibility: 'I've got this freedom. This is exciting. I can put up posters on the wall that I thought I couldn't, I can choose the washing powder he hated, I can drink his dusty bottles of expensive wine, one day I'll be able to date a new man.' She even got a new 'amazing' kitten for her and the children, now that her allergic ex is out of the picture. Most of all she credits an 'army of family and friends' and a network of women sharing similar experiences for helping her through the tough times. One WhatsApp message read, 'I'm six months ahead of you in the process. I know where you're at. You're gonna be OK. This is the shit bit. But every day will get better.'

When comic and storyteller Sarah Bennetto went through the worst of a series of breakups with the same person, she received a text from her friend, *The Guilty Feminist* podcaster Deborah Frances-White, saying, 'I'm in an Uber and I'm on my way over. I have a plan.' The plan involved sitting in Sarah's bed with her unpacking a large hamper of Ben & Jerry's, mint Aero bars and every treat she had ever mentioned that she loved.[2] Sarah also took up swimming and enjoyed the meditative state of 'not thinking any more'. Scientifically speaking, both of these were pretty sound plans.

Anna Machin suggests that the all-important opiate beta-endorphin, the one we have been plunged into withdrawal from after a breakup, is produced by lots of things completely unassociated with romantic love: 'So we could enhance these levels through exercise, dancing, singing, laughing with friends[3]...all those things will help. Or chocolate releases dopamine so that's good too. Or if you've got a cat or a dog, give them a stroke because that will release oxytocin.'

Exploring creativity can also be a healthy outlet. When performance poet Sophia Blackwell's relationship ended during her late twenties, she

---

2 Helen Thorn received a sort of budget version of this when a friend dropped off a packet of cigarettes and an Easter egg.

3 Hanging out with friends is definitely a great idea, whether heartbroken or not. *But* it is a bit more complex if you are gay. Most likely, your friends are friends with your partner too. Straight women are lucky in this regard. There's a bit more distance between their 'girlfriends', as in friends who are girls, and their boyfriends. They can get together with said friends and blame all their hurts and ills on men. They can have a celebratory, nurturing alliance free of the complexities of sexual attraction. Yet gay women don't quite have this place of safety.

felt unable to talk about it to her colleagues at her day job in publishing. Her evenings drifting around late-night clubs in Soho seemed a world away from their settled domesticity. So she wrote a journal which eventually became a novel. She went from an 'ephemeral' experience of 'living moment to moment', with 'poor short term memory' and an inability to settle on anything, to waking up in the early hours one night and having a sudden realisation that…she was over it. Writing about loss had helped her to dig herself out of its treacherous gully. Meanwhile, Elf Lyons remembers 'dancing around in her knickers painting in her mum's studio' in the wake of an early heartbreak. And I dusted off my guitar and had a go at playing through some of my old songs and teaching myself new covers when I was living on my own for a little while before meeting Girlfriend.

Although I initially thought the idea of a breakup haircut[4] seemed like only a very superficial rebirth, it does seem to hold some symbolic resonance for many of us. It harks back to historic rituals of cutting cords, ties, ropes or ribbons and removing bad spiritual energy, old emotions, patterns and thoughts. Apparently Coco Chanel once said that 'a woman who cuts her hair is planning changes in her life'.[5] Mind you, men are at it too. Lenny Kravitz shed his famous dreadlocks when he split with Vanessa Paradis in the 1990s.

And, finally, for women in particular, the old cliché that 'time heals' might at least have *some* truth.[6] A 2008 study published in the *Journal of Experimental Social Psychology* found that people bounced back from breakups about twice as fast as they predicted they would. Meanwhile, a 2015 Binghamton University study found that women reported higher levels than men of both physical and emotional pain immediately after a breakup. However, they recovered much better in the longer term.

Sometimes I wonder if we fragile humans are like machines that need to be reprogrammed every so often, the recovery period after a

---

4   Heartbreak can also sometimes cause hair loss if the immune system attacks the follicles. I, meanwhile, have had the same haircut for nearly thirty years…ever since I recovered from Kevin, Ormskirk's first bisexual hairdresser, giving me a free perm so that he could put a photo of it in the window at his shop De-Ziners. It was like a huge mushroom on top of my head and only served to further ostracise me at school.

5   See chapter 9! I should've known that The Bisexual Comedian was up to something when she had her hair cut off before buggering off to Cannes and leaving me in limbo.

6   Although it's super-annoying when people say it.

breakup akin to an essential software upgrade. After an emotional crash, we plug ourselves in and update. And we emerge improved.

Philosopher Alexander Nehamas suggests that the very fragility of human relationships is what makes them feel so precious. The risk is what renders them so rewarding. In the play *Sex with Robots and Other Devices*, one man duplicates an ex in order to relive one magical night over and over again. But surely what might initially seem like a utopia would turn into the most restrictive of groundhog days? Without the sadness of a breakup, how can we ever truly appreciate the happiness of being together? How can we ever develop and learn?

Even though Girlfriend and I drift apart sometimes, our wires crossed, our signals encrypted, our radar blips passing one another in the distant dark, we always seem to find our way back together. For now, and I hope for a very long time, we are one another's happy ending.

29

Happy Endings

Staying Together Stories: Nat Luurtsema

Nearing the end of recording the first live episode of season two of *The Breakup Monologues*, perched on the front edge of a roomy black leather armchair onstage in the intimate St Pancras Room at Kings Place, I ask both of my guests what a 'happy ending' would look like for them.

Sajeela Kershi, happily and defiantly single, tells me that she recently said to a friend, 'What I really want is for someone to have tidied the flat and made me a cup of tea when I come home. Maybe they'd brush my hair and I could cry on their shoulder.' Her friend said, 'You know what you need. You need a carer.'

But it is the story that emerges from my other guest, writer, director and comedian Nat Luurtsema, that surprises me…

'This is very romantic and also not very romantic…

'I knew my boyfriend was really special when we'd been together just four days.

'I should say that I commit really quickly. I probably should've got a dog a long time ago so I could be like, "Mr Muffin, you're my *one*." But anyway, I had a date with this guy, woke up at his flat and didn't leave…*ever*.

'And after we'd been together four days, I went for a sexual health test. As you do.

'And I was diagnosed with syphilis.

'The nurse said, "Don't google it, whatever you do. We think that it's historical syphilis and you've had it for more than ten years. So we need to scan your brain."

'When I was wondering whether to tell my boyfriend, my mum said, "Don't tell him."'

'But I can't keep a secret. So I met him outside his work. And I blurted out, "I've got syphiiiiilllllliiiiissssssssss" right on the steps of where he works, as people were leaving.

'So he cooked me dinner and gave me a hot water bottle. Remember we didn't know the symptoms because I'd been told not to google it. So every time I was like, "My tummy hurts" or "My feet are cold", we thought it was the syphilis.

'I went back to the clinic a week later for a counselling session… because it's such a bad illness to have.

'And apparently it was a misdiagnosis.

'But my boyfriend was so incredibly nice about it. He was so non-judgemental, which is more than I can say for the nurse who had asked all kinds of questions like, "Have you been having sex with circus folk?"

'And because he was so nice, that's my happily ever after. I knew he was a keeper.'

There's something so warm and special about the atmosphere in the room, full of laughter and joy. Carly Smallman and Sooz Kempner have snuck in ready to record their episode after the interval. I'm in my element in a gang I feel a legitimate part of. My guests are carefully chosen, partly because they're great acts but also because I like them as human beings.

Girlfriend is tipsily heckling, having been led astray by Becky. Angie has managed to pour white wine all over herself, trying to sneak an open bottle in. Meanwhile Liz arrives, chaotically late as usual, and sweetly acknowledges how much work I'm doing to make sure the door staff, sound engineer, photographer and guests are all OK. She says, 'You're like a duck swimming serenely on the water as far as most people are concerned. But I can tell that you're paddling away like fuck underneath the surface to make everything come together so well.' She's right. It's rewarding for me that a fellow creative notices the work that goes into making these events run smoothly. I am far from acquiring the list of TV credits that purports to be a badge of success as a comedian these days. But the eighty people that are here at my event are having a brilliant time. And a few thousand more around the world will enjoy listening to the podcast. I have found a way to combine humour and thoughtfulness in exactly the way I was hoping to, without compromising my artistic integrity. That feels like success to me.

Writer Abigail Tarttelin turns up with friends and we have a chat in the interval. She tells me that sharing her story on the podcast was the first time she had ever publicly spoken about her dramatic breakup.[1] 'It was so cathartic,' she says, 'I'm even writing a new book about that experience now.' I smile, feeling that perhaps there has been a real purpose to my quest. People really have found it helpful to share and swap stories.

The next day, I decide to message a few other friends to ask what their 'happily ever after' might look like. Louise Leigh says, 'To me, it feels like a conversation. After twenty years with my other half, it's a feeling of not wanting the conversation to stop, even when it repeats and repeats.' Facebook friend Silvia Dee says, 'Maybe it is committing to be with someone and honouring their personal evolution, sticking with it even when you could murder them over the toast just for breathing. Maybe it's being kind, finding the humour during testing times and *liking* as well as loving them.' Meanwhile, Pippa Evans suggests that she demonstrates her true love by not seeking to cash in on her husband's life insurance policy: 'I would be totally sorted financially. But instead I'm going to make my life much harder by not killing him.'

For the first time in months, I chat with Boozy Ex-Girlfriend. These days she is really quite sensibly in control of her alcohol intake and her moniker feels a tad unfair. She married a woman from Tasmania, after popping over to Sydney 'for a long weekend'[2] for their first date. In the wake of a big breakup, she assumed that online flirting with someone so far away would just be a bit of harmless fun. But it proved to be far more serious. They split their time between hemispheres and say that their 'happy ever after' is 'loving someone completely and them loving you just as much, just as you both are.'

And finally, I ask Girlfriend. Without hesitation she says, 'I'm in it!... I mean, there are things I could add like retiring early or having money to travel...But relationship-wise, I'm in my happy ending with you...if only I could get you to sleep with me sometimes!'

---

1   The one involving a car accident in LA. See Bite-Sized Breakup Stories in the middle of the book for details!

2   Who the heck 'pops over' to Sydney for a long weekend? It takes about a weekend just to get there!

30

We're Gonna Need a Bigger Bed

2 years 10 months A.G (After Girlfriend)

'Why are you being so difficult? Don't you want to sleep with me?'

I have been sighing around the bed shop, Dreams on Bromley High Street, sullenly dragging my feet like a moody teenager. I'm transported back to an occasion when I was taken out by Mum on a shopping trip to Southport to buy school shoes for the new term. I was perfectly happy with my scuffed old ones. On that occasion, I was able to curtail the undesired outing because I started my periods in the toilets at Broadbents. Mum had only just finished hers. An inconvenient baton of womanhood had been passed on. We drove home, me with a paper tissue in the gusset of my knickers. No such luck this time. Girlfriend is determined. She wants a new bed, a luxurious roomy one that will lure me back up to the top floor away from my independent dreams and cosy cuddles with Cat.

If we get a bigger bed, there will no longer be an excuse. There will no longer be a practical reason to not sleep together. Damn. It's not that I don't want to have sex with Girlfriend or to cuddle her or be close. I want all of those things. But I also want to hold onto the precious psychological space that I've been enjoying. Our relationship has improved since we occasionally started sleeping apart. We are just that little bit less tired. I don't want to be pressured back into bed together by a daft societal script that says it's what couples are *supposed* to do.

A man beckons us over to lie on a machine he seems disproportionately proud of. Two halves of a robotic double bed measure us and our movements and calculate exactly what mattress we need. I am hoping some kind of warning light will flash up a message that we are to avoid sharing a bed at all costs.

I lie stiffly on my back, a bit like the petrified position I adopted when a school friend I had a slight crush on asked me to stay over after a party and share her teenage single bed. I turn my head to face Girlfriend, bringing my elbow up at right angles to squash the foamy pillow out of the way and softly say, 'I love you. I'm with you forever. It makes sense to get a bigger bed. But what makes logical sense doesn't always make *psychological* sense. We've been feeling happy and sleeping well. Do we really want to change everything?'

She gets it.

'Bloody hell, baby. It's not for us to sleep together every night. I'm enjoying sleeping well too. I'd just like to have the option to feel close to you sometimes.'

'Oh, OK, that's fine then. I thought you meant *every* night.'

'God, no!'

'Oh haha, OK. Let's buy it.'

When we get home, I cook a huge cheesy fish pie for a late lunch with Angie, Liz and Nice Ex-Girlfriend. After a walk in the woods with Dog, conversation turns to my recent return visit to the sex lab. I had to sit through all the same clips, in a different order this time at least. Second time around, however, I have come away with some useful information. Luke shared some of his findings with me. Turning to Girlfriend, I announce, 'We thought we were bad gays for occasionally thinking about cock. But it turns out we aren't. The study has shown that only 30 per cent of women who define as lesbian actually demonstrate what they call a "masculine specificity of desire".'

'What does that mean?'

'They mean that straight men tend to be turned on by looking at women rather than men. And gay men tend to be turned on by looking at men not women…whereas, apparently, straight and bisexual women are turned on by both. I think they assumed that lesbians would be like straight men.'

'Yawn off,' says Girlfriend, unimpressed at this lazy assumption.

'…But what they've actually discovered is that the majority of lesbians are turned on by everything…just like straight and bisexual women.'

'Sounds about right,' giggles Liz.

'They can't find what differentiates us. It's not about whether the woman defines as butch, or is a gold star lesbian or has finger lengths that correspond to high levels of testosterone or anything. None of it correlates. We are just a bit mysterious.'

'I'll drink to that. I like being mysterious,' says Angie, tossing her hair coquettishly and raising her glass for a toast.

I don't think I particularly mind being mysterious either, now that I know I'm not alone in it.

With so many of my questions about sexuality and heartbreak beginning to be answered, I feel an unfamiliar calm. My quest may be nearing its end.

There will be another quest soon.

But for now, I can sleep…

'Where have you gone to?'

Girlfriend interrupts my half dream, hovering over me as if checking for vital signs. She smells clean and ready for bed as she scoops around me. I have passed out horizontally across the bed with all of my clothes on.

'God sorry, I was gone then.'

'Everyone seemed on good form today. Even Angie and Liz seem really happy together.'

'Yeah, they really did.'

'Wanna sleep up here tonight? We can practise ready for when the new bed arrives?'

I'm feeling so ridiculously comfortable in her arms that I can't contemplate standing up and moving to another room. Dog considerately spends much of the night in her own bed on the floor.

Epilogue: Love in the Time of Corona

3 years 5 months A.G. (After Girlfriend)

'I'm really glad you're doing this online Zoom gig tonight.'

'This one is just a bit of a pilot. I'm not getting paid.'

'Oh, I know. But it's good to just give it a go.'

'Yes, I suppose it might get my creative juices flowing.'

'Yeah…that…and it'll mean that you'll wash your hair and put makeup on.'

During my final months of writing this book, the UK is plunged into lockdown due to the coronavirus pandemic. The changes to society and how we can interact are unprecedented. Early suggestions from sociologists are that the pandemic has completely reshaped our close relationships. In every country that has had a lockdown, divorce rates have surged. Perhaps that is no surprise. Divorces normally peak just after holiday seasons at Christmas and summertime when people have had no escape from one another.

Meanwhile, video dating is becoming a new trend among singletons, with camera shunning, call screening and falsely blaming a poor internet connection becoming the latest forms of ghosting.

Girlfriend and I are incredibly lucky. Our families are healthy. And we have enough money to live on. For us, staying at home is not a hardship. It is a joy.

So while the deadly reasons behind social distancing seem too terrible to dwell on, this new silence feels golden – literally so as we walk Dog in deserted fields on glorious spring days. As we listen to a woodpecker drilling a tree, the kind of sound that is typically drowned out by the pace of twenty-first century life, I celebrate having an abundance of time and headspace to enjoy being in love. It feels like a gift to lie in bed until seven thirty or eight, even on a weekday morning, tracing the temporary creases left in her skin by the indentations of the pattern of the pillow.

Every Saturday night we chat to our friends. It's more regular contact than usual, albeit via video call. Even Angie and Liz seem loved-up, more stable and settled than ever before, laughing and joking in this opportune time out from the stress and scrutiny of normal life. It's good to see them this way. Perhaps those anti-love drugs won't be necessary after all.

Becky ponders whether to move in with her new lover. Meanwhile, Lena navigates the complexity of virtual sex and dating during self-isolation. Our friendships with both remain intact. Thank goodness Girlfriend talked me into politely postponing Lena's appearance on the podcast, a decision made all the more urgent when Becky revealed that she had bought tickets. Perhaps there's an appropriate sensitive gap to leave before interviewing friends about breakups with people we know.

One morning, while Girlfriend is out running, I revisit Kathy's list of reasons to break up and wonder if I am now in a position to convert it into a list of reasons to stay:

Sexual problems: I'll be honest. There's a sliver of sadness in my heart when I think that Girlfriend and I will probably never recapture the thrill of our first sexual encounters. The chemical high triggered by being with a new person seems near-impossible to replicate. It's not much to do with the sexy things that new person is doing with you in the physical realm. Not for me, at least. It's more to do with the psychological future that this person represents: 'I might feel less alone in the world after all.' And once that future becomes the present, we start to take it for granted.

But I will always have the memory of what it was like in the early days. And I know it wouldn't be like that with just anyone.

And sometimes that energy can be rekindled, particularly when we've had a little space, like the time I returned from a long weekend away in Berlin or when we've been hunkered down, focussed in on intensive work projects in separate rooms of the house for days. Sometimes there's a sense of newness when we come back together after feeling energised by work, separate interests or friends…particularly if we are able to settle Dog down in another room with the TV on and a treat.

And it doesn't seem to matter so much if several weeks go by without much in the way of wild sex. Because we have an almost constant supply of other intimacies – kisses, hugs, cuddles and holding hands. We touch one another in non-sexual ways all the time. I can't imagine having such an easy tenderness with anyone else. It seems worth compromising on wall-to-wall intense excitement if it means living a more contented and functional life overall. If I ever miss the extreme euphoria I once knew so well, I remind myself of the sadness and rage that counterbalanced it.

Incompatibility around money: At the beginning, our differing attitudes to money were a significant threat to the relationship. As a creative freelancer, I can get incredibly fretful over unpaid invoices and requests for me to work for free. I rarely treat myself to clothes or nice things just in case I have a rough patch. I was becoming so careful that I lost sight of how I could be earning much more.

Meanwhile Girlfriend openly describes herself as 'spendy'. She is the first person I've met who can have a fifty-quid blowout just on biscuits. They were really posh biscuits. But still!

When we began dating, I knew I couldn't keep up with her. But over time we met somewhere in the middle. I have learned to ask politely and respectfully for proper payment for my work. I have been able to discover better paid performing, speaking, writing and broadcasting opportunities, and find grants and funding I might not have had the confidence to apply for previously. Conversely, Girlfriend occasionally compares prices and looks for deals, rather than just assuming that the most expensive thing will always be the best. This gives her a chance to create a spreadsheet, always one of her favourite pastimes.

Domestic issues arising from living together: Since lockdown, we have become so much better at living together. Being around all day makes it easier to see who's doing what, divide up tasks equally and do some of the more fun ones, like cooking or walking the dog, together.

And having to plan shopping trips more strategically, rather than queue for an hour just to buy bread, makes me truly appreciate Girlfriend's organised lists. When things return to some kind of normal, I think we will remember this time and how skilled we became at negotiating. Having pets also makes living together way more enjoyable. They fill a home with love.

Drug and alcohol addiction: This one is not a problem for us. We are both rubbish at drinking. We have one glass of wine or champagne at a wedding and are enjoyably off our faces for a short time, then ready to switch to herbal tea at the first available opportunity.

Untreated mental health conditions: We have both experienced grief, so seem able to support one another when sadness rears its head. She seems to understand how to negotiate the eccentric way that my brain works. And I am able to handle her hormonal mood swings. Whether these technically count as mental health conditions I don't know. But these quirks can certainly lead to more serious mental health conditions when the people surrounding you misunderstand them. Fortunately, we have each other now.

Abuse (physical, verbal or emotional): Even when our arguments get heated and upsetting, there's never anything violent or cruel about them. We are so incredibly lucky. Many of our friends are not. For some of them, the real recovery is from the trauma of having been *in* the relationship in the first place rather than from eventually escaping it.

Conflicts over autonomy and intimacy: This is a complex one for me. When I'm single, I tend to feel more confident, sexy and assertive. I like myself more. When I'm forced to do things out in the world on my own, I am reminded how competent I actually am. These positive energies usually linger for the highly charged initial months of a new love affair, yet can dissipate rather disappointingly as I become part of 'the couple'. It feels like the individual I was before, the identity I had carved out so carefully, becomes incrementally less visible, even to my own friends. All of the people I like the most are somehow complicit in my erasure. This can result in pushing even the nicest of admirers away. Girlfriend is the first partner I've verbalised these struggles with. There's something about sleeping separately most nights that restores and recharges my sense of self just about enough to be blissfully happy as a fully engaged part of a couple the rest of the time.

Having experienced each of these issues as problematic in greater or lesser ways in previous relationships, I was better equipped to seek out the right partner for me. And I'm better able to recognise how good we have it. Without each of my breakups, and without thinking about them deeply, I wouldn't be where I am right now. Perhaps this obsessive quest was a worthwhile one after all.

I have previously compared our journey through our romantic relationships to video games or spinning plates. Perhaps it is also like stepping stones across a river. Sometimes we step on a really slippery, treacherous rock. It looked safe to begin with. But when you got there, it wasn't. When we fall, our confidence is knocked. Sometimes we have to take small steps for a while before we risk a big leap onto another big rock. But the leap we make after a fall is often the greatest one of all. Now I'm basking in the sun on a huge sturdy rock where I will stay a while.

As I complete my list, my eyes wander from the desk over to the bed where Dog and Cat are lying sleeping together. Cat extends a front paw over her eyes to block out the late morning sun. She rolls over drowsily to be almost touching Dog, in closer proximity than she would ever consciously allow. I stealthily take a photo on my phone, a reminder of this heart-warming moment of cuteness. Downstairs, I hear the sound of Girlfriend's key in the door as she returns panting and hot from her run.

'I'm home!'

Me too.

Conclusion: How Breakups Keep Us Together[1]

Kintsugi or Kinsukuroi is the Japanese art of repairing broken pottery with a lacquer mixed with powdered gold. The philosophy treats the breakage and repair as something to highlight rather than to disguise, a valid part of the object's history. Similarly, our breakups are vital parts of our personal growth, badges to be worn with pride rather than shame. If we can harness their potential by viewing them as opportunities for learning and healing, breakups can make both our future individual selves and our future relationships stronger.

Perhaps if we can share stories and appreciate that we are not alone in our heartbreak, we can comfort one another. Our brains are in shock. We are withdrawing from an intoxicating drug. Yet, in time, we will heal. Telling our story over and over, particularly among the comfort of friends, might reduce the trauma attached to it. Let's hear and soothe one another, eat chocolate, dance, exercise and laugh together. And maybe even cut off our hair, go travelling, start new careers and reinvent

---

1 I really wanted 'How Breakups Keep Us Together' to be the subtitle for the whole book. I thought it would signal my intention to be a little bit positive and uplifting about breakups. My editor thought it was a bit of a spoiler. Fair enough. But I still had to get it in somehow.

ourselves. Let's revel in new freedoms. We can't know true joy without having had a little jeopardy.

As we live much longer lives and are surrounded by so many dating options, we will go through breakups. It's a fact of life. Even many species of birds 'divorce' if one member of a pair arrives back at the breeding territory earlier than the other. They can't afford to wait. Their former mate could be injured or dead. They pair up with a new mate. They are just playing the odds.

Maybe we humans are simply playing a numbers game too, constantly swiping and browsing, or constantly weighing up our frustrations with a partner against their good qualities. Our decision to stay is based around a primal equation. Am I happy more than I am sad? Yet before you give up and roll the dice again, remember that relationships take work. A recent study of over 11,000 couples, previously mentioned in chapter nineteen, revealed that relationship happiness has little to do with your partner's personality and far more to do with the nature of your partnership.

And if you have to leave, consider having a face-to-face 'exit interview'.[2] Psychologist Barry Lubetkin says, 'The greatest problem people have in breakups is lack of closure.' Although it may seem 'kinder' at the time, a soft breakup often hits harder. Ambiguity leaves room for impossible hope, and delays and disrupts that person's recovery. Even though there is no official code of conduct for dating, remember to treat others as you would wish to be treated yourself.

Whether you are male, female, trans, non-binary, gay, straight, bisexual, pansexual, polyamorous, monogamous, young, old or somewhere in between, I wish you all well in your relationships and in your breakups. It's been fun talking to you.

---

2   Clearly, there is a huge exception around abusive relationships. Many women have to flee violent men and need to start a new life in safety.

Acknowledgements

First, my thanks go to my agent Cathryn Summerhayes and my editor Matthew Lowing. Without their initial enthusiasm and encouragement, this book would never have happened. And to the rest of the brilliant team at Bloomsbury who worked on this project: Holly Jarrald, Katherine Macpherson, Alice Graham and Lizzy Ewer.

I am so incredibly lucky over the last few years to have become friends with the incredibly talented author, actress, musician and all-round fierce feminist force of nature that is Abigail Tarttelin. Her insightful feedback on my early drafts was instrumental in the editing process. Make sure you read her awesome books *Golden Boy* and *Dead Girls* as soon as you possibly can.

Special mentions go to *The Breakup Monologues* producer Dave Pickering, one of the world's most compassionate and ethical humans, and to all of the podcast guests and interviewees who shared their stories. Also to Tim Schoenert for his excellent proofreading skills, Katie Margaret Hall for her friendship and festival research, and to superstar role models and cheerleaders Jac Nunns and Ange West for supporting season four of the podcast.

Further thanks go to Arts Council England and Bradford Literary Festival for supporting the very first live pilot stages of *The Breakup Monologues* and to the British Podcast Awards and Wellcome for supporting the podcast mini-season *My Chemical Romance?* which provided the material for the chapter of the same name.

And a big shout out to my *Radio Diva* family – Heather, Rachel, Jonathan, Linda, Fiona, Carrie, Roxy, Danielle, Jacquie and Fizz.

Although the show is no more, I learned so much. The spirit of what we created lives on and continues to inform my work.

High fives to inspiring female creatives everywhere…especially to Viv Groskop who, despite juggling a phenomenal number of things, never seems too busy to tweet a supportive message about a colleague's work. To Kal Lavelle for kindly allowing me to reproduce some of the lyrics of her awesome song. To Kathy Labriola, Jacqui Gabb, Kate Leaver, Meg-John Barker and Sally Holloway for sending me copies of their books and allowing me to quote from their work. And to Jen Brister, who got onstage for an impromptu double act with me at the Women in Comedy festival when I was having a meltdown after my breakup with Nice Ex-Girlfriend.

Finally, of course, I'd like to send all my love to my darling Girlfriend. Every day is an adventure with you. Thank you for opening my eyes to so many things, not least to the brilliance of dogs.

Further Reading

- *Rewriting The Rules* by Meg-John Barker
- *The Secrets of Enduring Love* by Meg-John Barker and Jacqui Gabb
- *Love is the Drug* by Brian D. Earp and Julian Savulescu
- *Maybe You Should Talk to Someone* by Lori Gottlieb
- *The Curious History of Dating* by Nichi Hodgson
- *The Game of Love in Georgian England* by Sally Holloway
- *The Polyamory Breakup Book* by Kathy Labriola
- *The Friendship Cure* by Kate Leaver
- *Untrue* by Wednesday Martin
- *Wintering* by Katherine May
- *Love Factually* by Laura Mucha
- *Mating in Captivity* by Esther Perel
- *Out of the Woods* by Luke Turner
- *Conscious Uncoupling* by Katherine Woodward Thomas